SALT STORY

'a unique and atmospheric offering.' *Australian Book Review*

'a lyrical and utterly absorbing account of a fragile industry and a precarious way of life. [five out of five stars]' *Adelaide Advertiser*

'a thoroughly original mosaic of stories and atmospheric pieces' *Sydney Morning Herald, Saturday Age, Canberra Times*

'wry, poetic slices of life as a fisherwoman' *The Age*

catch of the day' *QANTAS the Australian Way*

'easy, flowing, and charming ... atrocious puns aside, I'm hooked' *The West Australian*

'intelligent and impassioned' *The Weekend Australian*

'warm, lively, salty account' *Good Reading Magazine*

'an important documentation of a living history ... intoxicating' *Kill Your Darlings*

First published 2013 by

FREMANTLE PRESS
25 Quarry Street, Fremantle 6160
(PO Box 158, North Fremantle 6159)
Western Australia
www.fremantlepress.com.au

Reprinted 2013.

Also available as an ebook.

Consultant editor Georgia Richter
Cover design Ally Crimp
Cover photograph istockphoto, franckreporter
Maps Chris Crook, Country Cartographics
Printed by Everbest Printing Company, China

National Library of Australia
Cataloguing-in-Publication entry:
Drummond, Sarah, author.
Salt Story: of sea-dogs and fisherwomen / Sarah Drummond.
ISBN: 9781922089069

Small-scale fisheries—Western Autralia—Great Southern Region—Anecdotes.
Fishers—Western Australia—Great Southern Region.
Women in fisheries—Western Australia—Great Southern Region.
Great Southern Region (W.A.)—Social life and customs.
305.96392099412

Government of **Western Australia**
Department of **Culture and the Arts**

lotterywest
supported

Australian Government

Australia Council
for the Arts

Fremantle Press is supported by the State Government through the Department of Culture and the Arts. Publication of this title was assisted by the Commonwealth Government through the Australia Council, its arts funding and advisory body.

SALT STORY

OF SEA-DOGS AND FISHERWOMEN

SARAH DRUMMOND

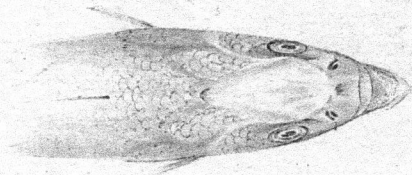

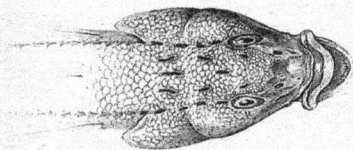

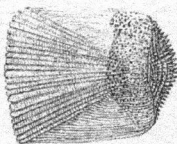

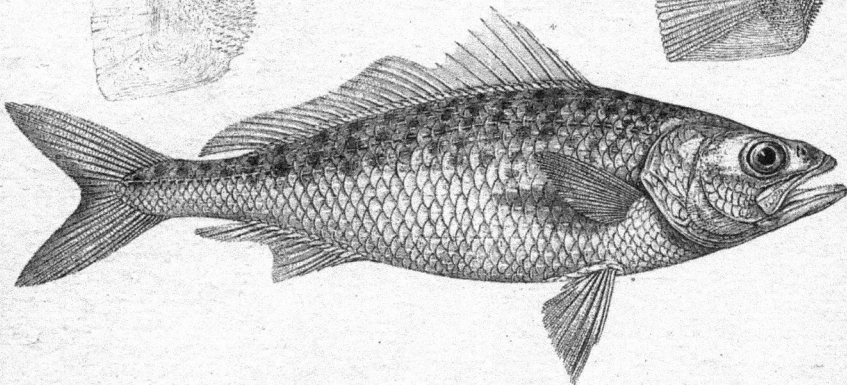

for Matilda Grace

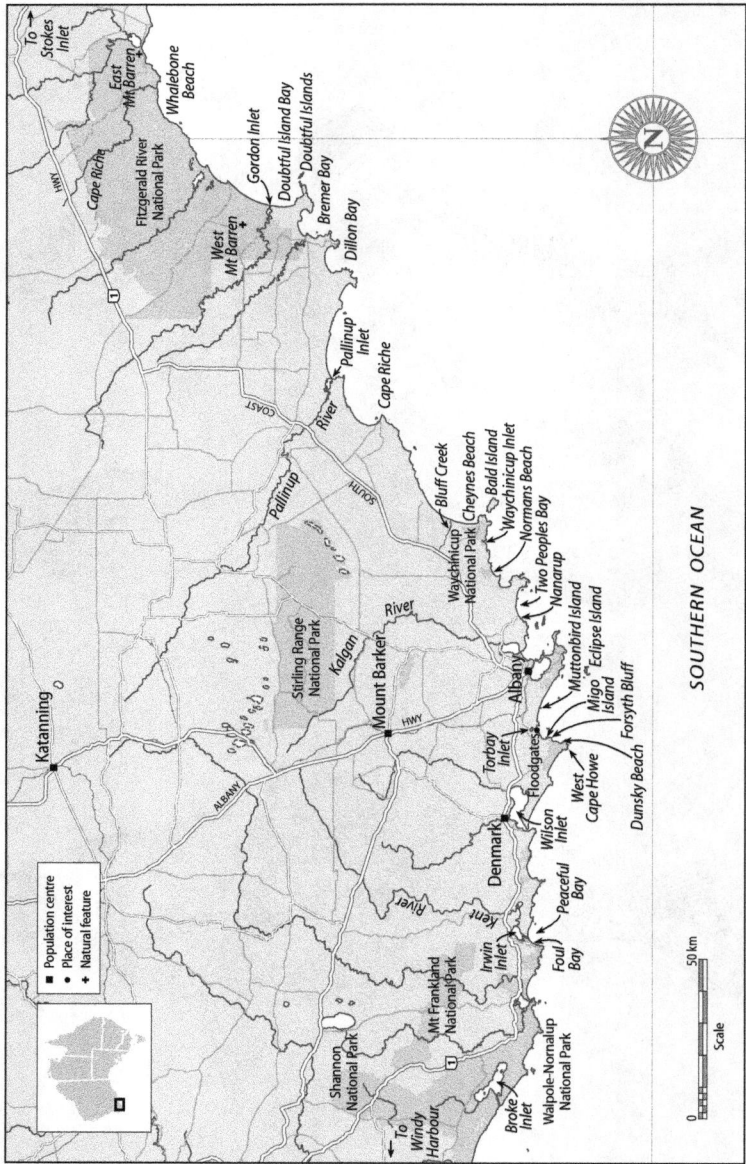

The Great Southern

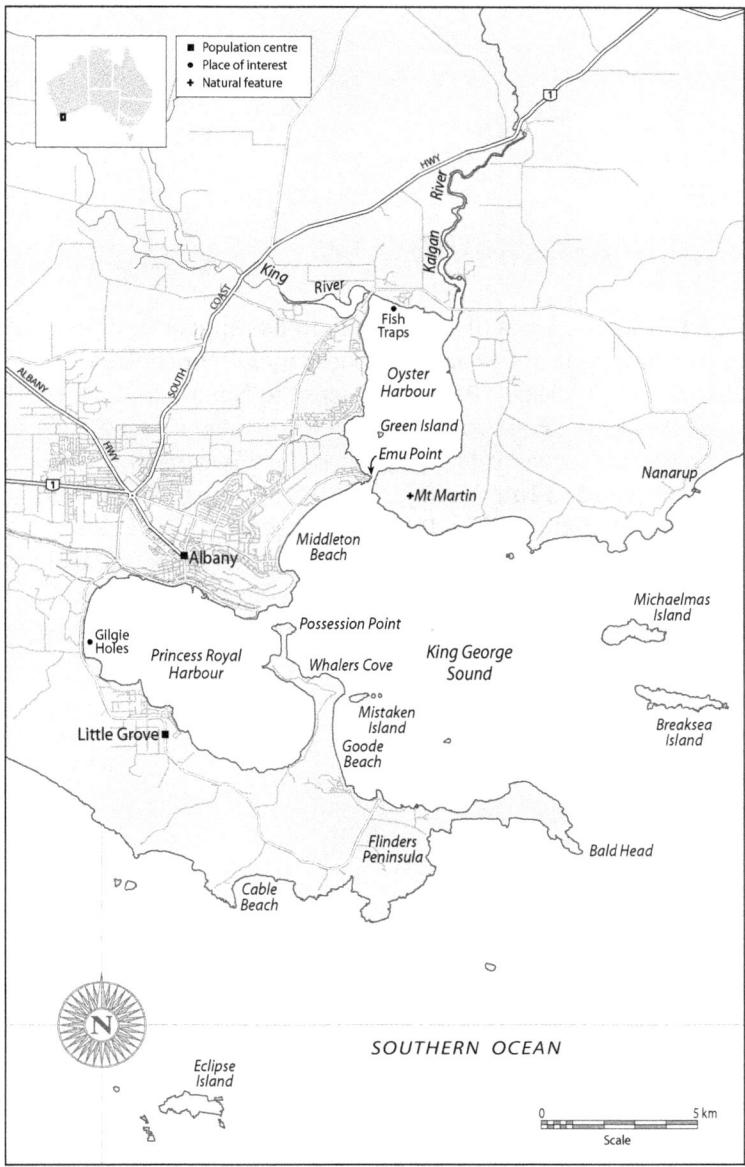

Legend:
- ■ Population centre
- ● Place of interest
- ✦ Natural feature

HWY

Kalgan River

King River

COAST

SOUTH

ALBANY

HWY

● Fish Traps

Oyster Harbour

Green Island

Emu Point

Nanarup

✦Mt Martin

Middleton Beach

■Albany

Michaelmas Island

● Gilgie Holes

Possession Point

King George Sound

Princess Royal Harbour

Whalers Cove

Breaksea Island

Mistaken Island

■ Little Grove

Goode Beach

Flinders Peninsula

Bald Head

Cable Beach

N

SOUTHERN OCEAN

Eclipse Island

0   5 km
Scale

Kinjarling (King George Sound and surrounds)

A NOTE REGARDING MAPS

Older or local names of places that do not appear on these maps, or appear under another name include: Brook's Inlet (Broke Inlet); Casey's Beach (adjacent to Nanarup); Cathedral Rock (at Windy Harbour); Irwin's (Irwin Inlet), Floodgates (adjacent to Torbay Inlet and Muttonbird Beach); the Gordon (Gordon Inlet); Kinjarling (King George Sound and surrounds); Pallinup (the Beaufort, Beaufort Inlet, Pallinup Estuary); Possum Point (in Irwin Inlet); Seal Rock (adjacent to Point King); Skippy Reef (off Possession Point); Wilson's, the Wilson (Wilson Inlet); Whalebone Beach (Doubtful Island Bay).

CONTENTS

SAME TRIBE AS ME
(AN INTRODUCTION)

Drawn on Stone by W. Mitchell.　　　　　　　　　Hullmandel & Walton Printers

SALT

He was burly and sad and smelled vaguely of mutton. He handed me an apple and talked about fish. 'They're not real salmon, y'know. That was Captain Cook's fault. He thought they looked a bit like a salmon and the name stuck. They're really a kind of overgrown herring.'

The old fisherman looked to me for a response. Folds of skin nearly obscured his eyes and scabby cancers colonised his nose. 'You eat an apple just like I do.'

'Core and all?'

'Yeah. Don't those seeds taste good?'

Salt Story was born in the Great Southern inlets and bays of Western Australia. Initially, these tales of fisher men and women may appear to read as fragments of a day, a life – ripping yarns, beautiful lies and a few home truths. But these sixty-two pieces contribute to a living history of the estuarine and inshore fishers. *Salt Story* is my tribute to the beauty and fragility of the industry.

Small-scale, inshore fishing on the wild south coast hasn't changed much in the last century. Aluminium boats with outboard engines have replaced a lot of the wooden carvels and clinkers, and fish find their fate meshed in nylon monofilament rather than heavy cotton nets tarred with grasstree resin. Trailered boats allow fishers to work estuaries further away, for shorter hours. Once a fisherman's whole family may have camped on the shores of Wilson Inlet for the six weeks that the mullet were running. Now he can drive out, set nets and make it home in time for dinner.

I first met Salt when I camped by the beach and helped his salmon team seine tons of the fish into shore. A pink and whiskery bloke, wearing a beanie, a pair of jocks and a jumper that stretched over an impressive beer gut, he sat aboard an ancient tractor and towed one end of the net up the beach. The net strained against the suck of the swell, full with thrashing salmon. Men, women and children held the net upright, heading off any fish that threatened to leap out. The six or seven dogs present managed to look concerned, excited and bored, all at once. When the fish were dragged up on the beach, Salt climbed off the tractor and stepped with thorny feet through the small sharks and salmon, grabbing stingrays by their mouths and throwing them back into the surf.

As a wayward teen, I found myself hanging around a lot of jetties and beaches. Beaches, piers and wharves reminded me of another point of arrival and departure – the roadhouses – where at night the neat red lights of the big rigs signified to me the will of a people removing themselves from housebound communities. The lot of fishermen, yachties and truckies seemed to be a purposeful shiftlessness, a nomadism that raised a middle finger to the myth of the Great Australian Suburban Dream.

'You never stray far from the sea, do yer,' said Salt, when I hatched my next project out loud. What was it again? Getting a berth on the anti-whaling crusader *Sea Shepherd*? Writing a biography of a Norwegian whale chaser? Maybe it was my plan to head down to Antarctica with the Patagonian toothfishermen for a season.

I have always wanted to hang out with these kinds of people. I want to understand them, to rub through the veneer of people who spend their lives on the water. I say 'veneer' because being away from land and then returning can produce a kind of aloofness. Land people will never understand what sea people are talking about. They are creatures from different universes.

Back in the days when Salt was still being nice to me, he said, 'Dunno girl. I just don't swear around women. Never have.'

How touching and old-fashioned, I thought.

It's funny how things slide. Aboard, Salt has the tongue of jellyfish tentacles. It is not a hasty generalisation to say that fishermen can swear a bit. So be warned, there is some 'language' in these stories.

The places we fish are the inlets and bays of the Great Southern: Broke Inlet, Irwin's, Pallinup Estuary or the Beaufort as it is also called, Oyster Harbour and Princess Royal Harbour, Waychinicup, Stokes, The Gordon, Wilson's, King George Sound and Two Peoples Bay. Some of the inlets are stone bound and permanently open to the sea. Others are closed by a sandbar until it rains enough. Then the rivers rush down from high country and the sea pushes in. Sometimes people bulldoze a channel, to save their cow paddocks, their road, their fishing shack or their sea-changer from the seasonal, watery annihilation as the inlet swells into the country. The inlets tend to sit behind a mound of sand-dune country. These are fertile, furtive places, protected from the open 'yang' roar of the ocean and onshore winds. They often seem to have their own climate, their own little raincloud hanging in the stillness, a cooling breeze ruffling the water, the reeds dripping with moisture and threaded with tiger snakes.

From fish traps and spears and cooking beneath the ground wrapped in paperbark, to netting the Pallinup estuary for mullet and bream and sending the fish in trucks to the Perth markets, the south coast inlets and bays hold stories about men and women within them: the fugitives, shell-shocked hermits, bird lovers and salmon-fishing families. The fishers told me stories about their ancestors, some of whom have fished this coast for five generations. They mostly work at night or in the dawn hours and tend to keep to themselves.

Theirs is an existence which is challenged today by constant wrangles with government departments over licensing, industry reviews, and the uncertainties presented by proposed marine parks. Some south coast fishermen think of themselves as an 'endangered species' and, considering the social and political pressures, popular anxieties about overfishing and friction between commercial and amateur groups, it's not an unreasonable status. In some countries the commercial fishers are a valued part of their nation's cultural heritage but this is not always so in Australia.

Salt Story tells of netting with Salt in a little tinny in the southern waters of Western Australia, and of some of the other fishers who work the same grounds: sea-dogs, fisherwomen, tough guys, oystermen and storytellers.

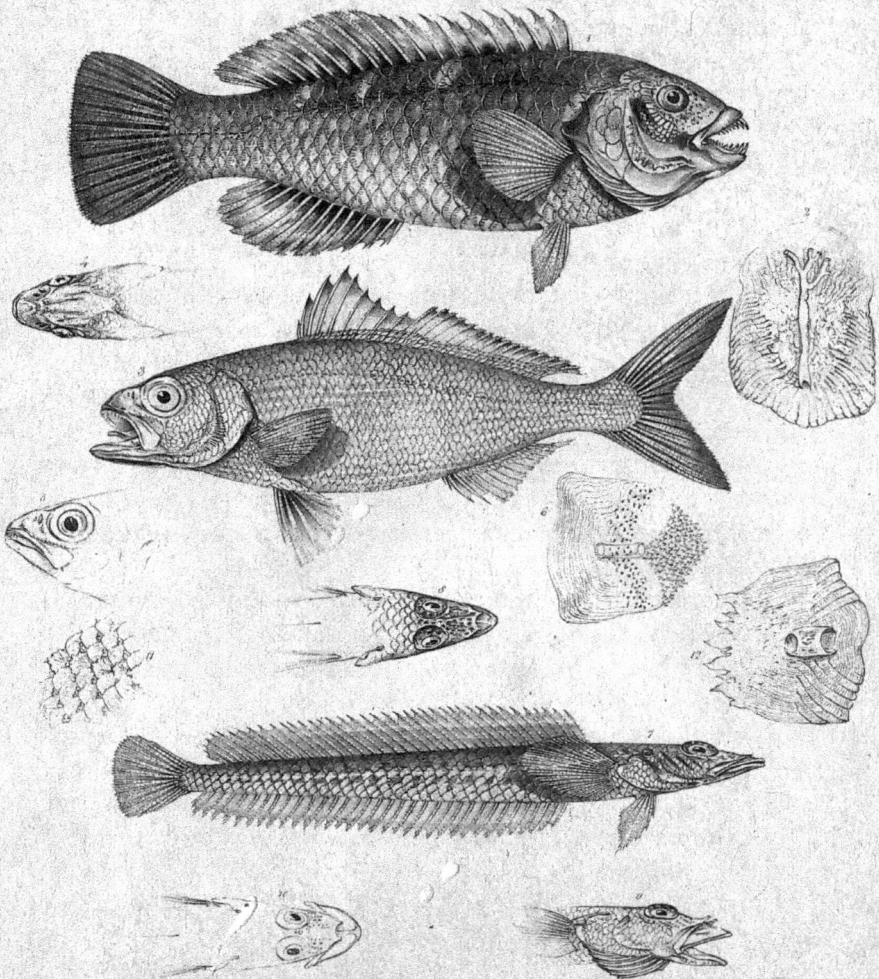

MASTER'S APPRENTICE

Working for Salt involves no contracts, few rules and sometimes I get the feeling this apprenticeship will never end unless one of us dies or I manage to snare myself a Fisheries officer for a husband. I've quit twice and he's sacked me once but come the next week, we are always back out on the water.

THE NET THAT DOESN'T CATCH ANYTHING

'What have we got? A brick fish!' We haul up the house brick that holds the net to the ocean floor.

'Nuffing!' Salt shakes his head in disgust. He says it every time we pick up that brick. 'Fuckin' nuffing.'

There is a legendary flathead lurking somewhere in King George Sound. I hear about it quite a lot. 'It just ate that KG,' Salt growls, tearing a mangled King George whiting from the mesh.

'Not a stingray?'

'Nah, it's that big fuckin' flathead. Too big to fit in the box, it is. About the size of a small crocodile but nastier.'

If you told me the word gullible wasn't in the dictionary, I'd have to check, secretly, later. 'Really?' I ask, agape. 'Have you seen it?'

'Seen it? It tried to chew me leg off,' he pulls up his wet-weather pants to show me the scar. It is a terrible scar, two sets of teeth marks, scoring across to meet in the middle of his calf.

'But wasn't that a shark?' Last time he showed me that scar, he said a dog shark had latched onto his leg and he'd had to cut off its head because, in all the excitement, the shark's jaws locked.

'Nah, that's the other leg, girl,' he smirked. 'Great night at the Bremer Bay pub that night. The barmaid had to fetch the pliers onto me.'

In the early evening, the western wind turbines slowed and then stopped.

'Not far now. We're nearly onto The Net That Doesn't Catch Anything,' Salt says.

'It's not so bad, that net.'

'Nope. I'm cutting it off tomorrow. Forgot to do it today. Doesn't catch anything,' Salt says. The silver gleam of King George whiting flash into the plastic bins. 'And it's too shallow. Pike swim straight over the top.' Just like that, there is a pike, then two, three, wrapped up in mesh like a rolled roast and still baring their teeth. 'I'm gonna cut the whole lot off. It's useless. It's The Net That Doesn't Catch Anything.'

Salt has diamonds on the soles of his feet tonight, electric blue, phosphorescent diamonds.

'Take me home.' He sits amidships on the pile of nets and looks ahead as I take the tiller. Just like a working horse, it is my favourite time of day but not because I am going home. It's nearing ten at night and the wind has dropped. We have the loveliest tub of fish for tomorrow's market. Navigation lights – green, red, yellow, blue – blink around me. I head into the channel and feel the chill of the land. The woodchip mountain is composting, woody scented. Steam clouds the orange lights. Our crocodilian wake flickers with fire in the water.

We never say anything during this part of the trip, not just because of the noisy two-stroke. It is that short period of absolute satisfaction that everything is right with the world.

'I'm gonna get on the piss soon,' Salt tells me at the jetty. 'Been too good for too bloody long. I'm gonna go out and shake this town up, shake things up a bit. It's about bloody time.'

He's pretty happy. He's outfoxed that fisherman's jinx yet again. It's been a good night's fishing, despite that net.

SELECTIVE HEARING

One of the Aunties told me that she and the grandies swam a net out at Pallinup, and caught all this sea mullet. I mentioned it to Salt and the next time he saw her, he had to ask. 'Where'd you catch that mullet?'

'Oh, over by the bar. Then we set another net, caught some more, cooked it up on the beach wrapped in paperbark.'

'Which beach? What side of the bar?' He listened intently to her directions.

Salt has been itchy about sea mullet, seeing as the latest theory is they've swum up the Pallinup River where we commercial fishers are not allowed to work. So we were out on the inlet this week trying to find where this woman had caught her fish. The evening was so still and clear that as we planed across the inlet, it felt the boat wasn't even moving, just the sky and the red cliffs moving towards us. We set two overnight nets by the paperbarks near the bar, where furtive camp fire smoke smudged the trees.

The next morning it was raining sideways. That was the first bad thing. I kept shouting to slow down as we roared out to the nets because the rain was drilling me and I hadn't found my sunglasses in the half-dark tent. As we hauled in the net, I began to realise we'd started at the wrong end. Salt had to start the motor again and reverse along it because the wind was blowing the boat across the net and getting everything tangled.

I also understood that my wet-weather gear was no longer waterproof. The plastic had worn away from the lining when I'd left my pants and jacket pegged on the camp washing line during the storms. This may seem like a minor technicality but I was living in a tent at the time. Dodgy wet-weather gear in sideways rain when the nearest hot shower or clothes dryer is fifty kilometres away, is a *real bastard*.

Then Salt backed into the net and bound up the prop in monofilament. You know the Conchords song 'Business Time'? Yeah, well. It's Whingeing Time. Six in the morning, the sun not yet wakened and my expletives were already spraying the deck. Salt always thinks my tantrums are very funny, so to up the entertainment, he backed into the net a second time after I'd untangled the first one from the propeller.

It wasn't easy in that wind to climb over the stern of the dinghy with a filleting knife between my teeth, lean into the outboard and start fiddling with strands of nylon wound tight around the prop. Plus I was no longer waterproof. (Have I mentioned I wasn't waterproof?) Salt couldn't do the untangling because his waterproof waders severely constricted his movements.

'I know what's going on,' I shouted over the sleet, surf spray and other flying rhetoric. 'You've got a deckie! No one else has a deckie. If you didn't have a deckie, you'd be thinking about how to make your job easier. But no. No. You've got a fucking deckie.'

He looked a bit bemused, like when he can't hear me speaking, like when he just sees my mouth opening and shutting in the middle of a meaningless torrent of strange and vaguely humorous facial expressions. He looks like that a lot, when I start yelling.

BREATH OF THE WORLD ...

Massive schools of flathead swarm into the harbour in November, some laden with spring roe and feasting on anything in their way. After setting some raggedy net in our special spot, I jumped ship and explored the cairn-encrusted Possession Point. Towards her rocky peak were little gardens of perfect crimson orchids in emerald moss and verticordia, that flowered pink against the granite.

The sun began to slip away behind the wind turbine. I returned to the boat, where Salt leaned over the stern and stared into hypnotic depths. We drank coffee, peeled an orange each and waited for the night.

Beneath the boat, I could only imagine all the things going on, connected to these happenings by the net and what it would reveal. There was the skin of the water and Salt's boat, floating above this universe. Down there, flathead swam in toothy, carnivorous swathes and the eccentric little spider crab preened her new crown – a single length of seagrass. Turquoise grass whiting fled from the greedy spotted sharks and vampire bat rays. Strange currents ran beneath the calm surface, rolling the net into tight bundles of monofilament and weed. Seagrass undulated in rippling meadows and above all the drama, the dinghy fidgeted against her anchor like a naughty pony.

A swollen golden moon rose over Mount Martin and dwarfed a container ship that swung on its anchor, waiting. By the huge granite slopes on the channel, Gawain was checking his leatherjacket pots. He bent over the beam, his red anorak glowing in the fluorescent light.

The wind dropped.

Water heaved with the breath of the world.

We picked up the tangled nets, heads and fish rendered utterly unrecognisable. Stingray. The flathead of legend chose not to fall for the wily entreaties of Salt, again.

Staunch tugboats nudged the *Kwan Yin* into wharf timbers. A figurine of the goddess of compassion and motherhood once held pride of place on the dash of my car and now her namesake, this freighter, distributed superphosphate all over Earth.

Wheat silos, smooth white chrysalids, stood among the praying mantis gantry and chugging conveyor belts, orange lights, steaming mountains of woodchips, ships high on the water out in the Sound. All night, the port worked to clear the backlog. Ships in, ships out. Breathe in, breathe out.

The moon was huge, fecund and close to the earth. The ocean rose up to her siren song. After only a few hours fishing in the Sound, the water had swelled over the jetty planking and gently but forcefully, as water is wont to do, urged my return to land.

IT'S NOT ALL HALCYON NIGHTS AT SEA

'If anyone tells you they've never been frightened out of their wits at sea, they're lying,' Ms Mer once said to me. Ms Mer is a south-west fisherwoman who has spent most of her life at sea, so she should know what she's talking about.

No liar, me. When I get scared, I start to feel like an idiot, which in turn makes me grumpy. Despite my anxieties, there is no one I would feel safer with out on the water than Salt, and his faith in me is bolstering. In the first week of my apprenticeship, Salt gave me the tiller out near the islands, when even the night stars were blacked out by cloud, and said, 'There's *red port left*, girl. Let the lights take you home.'

One night in King George Sound a strong easterly blew and the wind waves as we hit the heads were ... well put it this way ... I would have liked a bigger boat. Every time a white-capped screamer aimed its malevolent slop at the gunwales, I'd turn the bow into it.

'Don't worry. You can take it on the beam with those puppies,' Salt smiled at me paternally and then cursed when the next spray drenched him. 'But you can take it on the bow if you really want to.'

We set some whiting nets out of the wind. I love that hour of waiting for fish to mesh and watching the sun go down. We laid up in the lee of Mistaken Island. I took off my wet-weather gear and asked Salt to drop me on the island. A charter yacht sailed through the channel and I heard the skipper shout a hello to Salt. The narrow channel surged with tide. In a rock pool that collects the flotsam from all over the Sound, I found some glass and a shard of ancient pottery. Perchance a pirate's rum jar?

Fairy penguins began their evening cries. I climbed aboard again and we sat, happy. I think we even had a beer. Then we motored over to the buoy.

'A seahorse! It's that time of year again.'

'Yeah, the spring racing season.'

Seahorses are difficult to unmesh in the half-light due to their hooked appendages but I've managed to persuade Salt that it is worth the time and effort to see them off alive. This one carried roe.

'What is it then – male or female?' Salt asked me.

'Dunno ... when does she hand them ova? Ha ha.' At some stage the male seahorse looks after the eggs. Salt wasn't sure when either.

'You know some fish are born male and turn female,' he said. 'Barra do that a lot.'

'Some people are born female and turn male.'

'Yes, but they've had append-dick-to-me's.' He cracked himself up at that one.

'Everyone is female to begin with ... brings a whole new meaning to your balls dropping.'

'That must mean us blokes are more evolved.'

'Well, as long as you blokes think that, then everything's okay.'

'Maybe that one is a night mare,' he says as I finally get the critter free and throw it into the sea. 'It is night, after all.'

This is the stuff we really talk about.

Water swilled around my bare feet. I heard a noise, like radio static.

'What noise?' said Salt.

He's quite deaf, Salt, but I could hear the water surging into the boat.

'The bung! There's no bloody bung!'

He thought this was hilarious.

I thought we were all going to die, or something.

'That's your fault, deckie. Deal with it.'

The squall from the south-west, that he'd been watching and commenting on, rolled in at precisely that moment. The boat was taking in water and the weight made her slew around and rock violently with every wave. We were halfway through fifteen hundred metres of net, so we couldn't throttle the motor to flush some of the water out. Sea began to slop over the stern.

'Bale, girl!' Salt handed me the bucket. 'There's no better bilge pump than a frightened deckie.'

We hauled up the rest of the nets, fish and all, water swilling around my knees. I cranked up the outboard and we charged across the Sound and into the harbour. Gradually the boat discharged her briny load. The waves pushed up by the squall squeezed into the channel against the outgoing tide, pushed the sea into unpredictable peaks. I screamed with mad, terrified laughter as we surfed that channel home.

THE EASTERLY OF MY DISCONTENT

I sat on a warmed rock at sunset. I sat there as a prospective mutineer, a female Fletcher Christian of the Deep South. I can handle all sorts of things. I can handle live sharks, cobbler, getting scared, getting wet and stingrays.

I can't handle that *damned onshore whore* – that incessant summer easterly – or sea lice. I get hysterical when sea lice drop off the fish and bite the webbing between my toes. There is nothing quite so gross. Salt has laughed at my screaming lice dance before but he grew quiet when I said they would crawl up his legs and into his bum and eat him from the inside out.

On summery full-moon nights there are lice aplenty and the easterly will not let up. Never say sagely to me, 'Oh, the wind will drop at sunset.' Another good one, if you really want the book of expletives thrown at you, is: 'Well, it's blowing onshore a bit at Goode Beach but we can set along the sandbanks for whiting and anyway – there's nowhere else to go.'

Nowhere else to go? Shipmate, it's Friday night.

At dusk we sat in the car and looked at Goode Beach. True to form, the easterly wind teamed up with the easterly swell and made a meat cleaver mess of the whiting grounds. Weed, slushy white caps and wind; one moment's inattention would see the tinny in the surf.

'Looks all right,' said Salt.

'Oh, for crying out loud!'

The best thing about Salt is that in gnarly situations he will never chuck a tantrum. Ever. That's my job. Because we are both seagoing Aquarians, an interesting kind of egalitarian tantrum relegation system has evolved within the highly structured workplace of the tinny. I chuck the tantrums and he don't give a shit.

Still, I got my way and we left the beach for the flathead grounds on the other side of the headland. Even out there, the wind swung over the hills and batted us into the harbour so the nets ended up all over the place.

Got wet. Set net.

Salt dropped me in a sheltered cove by Point Possession. He said he'd come back when it was time to pick up the nets and do the lice dance. I picked my way over the rocks, looking for polished glass among the smashed turban shells and periwinkles. I sat down on a rock and listened to the swell whacking up against the hill just behind me. I had my mobile phone. Maybe I could call for a helicopter, like a taxi. But really, I knew we had to get back out there and that it was going to be awful.

The phone beeped with a message.

Champers this eve. Didn't Salt tell you? X Rua.

Bastard.

'I told her you were coming fishing,' Salt said later.

'When?'

'Yesterday. I thought you'd prefer to come fishing.'

'Right.'

It blew harder as we neared the channel. Weird, sloppy waves peeled off Skippy Reef. So far, we'd caught two trumpeters, a poisonous spiked angelfish and two flathead. Salt motored along the net and I untangled any feeble morsels who were feeling depressed enough to choose suicide and mesh.

'Well, you can still go to her party.'

'Mmm. It's nearly ten o'clock. I'm soaking wet. I'm covered in trumpeter guts. I'm in the middle of Princess Royal Harbour and *I can't see my fairyfuckinggodmother anywhere!*'

WASHERWOMAN, FISHERWOMAN

It rained all day until people began to realise that it would flood. The main street of town turned into a river and the concrete stairs on Stirling Terrace were rubbled by the deluge. The publican at the White Star kicked out the drinkers early and started sandbagging. I saw a matronly patron dancing in the street. The taxi drivers watched her as slurry swirled around the axles of their cars.

I'd managed to stay on land, but far from dry, the night the southern spring hammered down five inches. I have to remind Salt often that I am a fairweather fisherwoman but these reminders rarely carry much authority. (About as much authority as a fisherwoman has in the Microsoft spellcheck universe it seems. Word has it that I am not a *fisherwoman* but a *washerwoman*.) Of course the weather was always my main concern with going fishing that night of the big rain. The red dress and the visiting minstrels at the White Star had absolutely nothing to do with anything.

On the morning before the flood, I talked with Snow and some other friends at the cafe about the nature of work and how we go about it. 'I know all these people who have bosses and are so unhappy,' he said. 'For others it is the perfect set-up. No responsibility. Go home at the end of the day … I couldn't stand it though. I've always worked for myself. It's the only way I can do it.' Then he told me that one of his jobs had been as a droog extra on the movie *A Clockwork Orange*.

We all stared at him. Snow was a droog? Far out!

My fishing income has eclipsed that of my other jobs and I

reckon that makes me a fisherwoman instead of someone who just goes fishing. Salt has been suggesting that I get some bins in my name. His reasoning is that when fishers present their wares at the city's fresh fish auctions, they get the best price with their first bin of fish and it degenerates from there. So, if we send up two names, we make more money per bin. That's Salt's logic. I just like the idea of sending bins of fish to Perth with my name on them. Fisherwoman. Yes.

I also like the Hemingwayesque element of my work, that beautiful interplay of art and labour, the cerebral marrying the physical. Writing about my other jobs as courier driver or kitchen hand never conjure up the same kind of whimsy. I find it hard to wax lyrical about consignment notes or the number of potatoes I've boiled in one afternoon. But to head out to the wine dark evening sea, to hear whales singing and see their phosphorescent meanderings and experience those occasions like the Night of the Flathead, when the boat threatened to sink under the freakish amount of fish we'd caught – that is a storyteller's paradise.

But this night the pot-belly clicked with heat and began to glow red. Lightning spread across the skies. There was a bottle of schnapps beside me. I knew Salt wanted to go fishing. My wet-weather gear was still wet and it looked like it was going to get even wetter. We hadn't made much money that week but looking outside at the skies made me feel quite flaky. I'm just not that tough. In fact, I was feeling decidedly girly in the best sense of the word – I had my red dress hanging by the fire to dry and I was trying to work out which pair of heels I liked best.

Salt rang again. 'The weather's easing up.'

'*It is not.*' I looked out the window to the south. Dammit. I liked this red dress and all its potential. Dammit. 'It's a dog's breakfast over this side of town,' I told him. 'There is no way I'm getting wet tonight.'

THE ART OF SEA-DOGGERY

Speaking of dogs, there is Digger. He is learning the art of sea-doggery.

He first came to live with me when his owner went up north for a 'few weeks', one year ago now. I was a dogsitter I suppose, and should have been paid lots and lots of money. It was generally after trips to the dentist that I came home to find he had pulled down a veranda post, utterly destroyed my favourite chair or rolled in some of the disgusting things that fisherwomen tend to bury in their gardens. Then it was time for the long-distance phone call, folding expletives around anaesthetised lips, 'Come and get this bloody dog! I do love him but my life is falling apart! My house is falling apart! ... what? Well put him on the plane then. *He's not my dog.*'

It became my refrain. '*He's not my dog.*'

People said, 'Oh, he's so lovable and cuddly.'

'*He's not my dog.*'

The fact that he is a seventy-kilo bull-mastiff slowed them down a bit, when I asked for their phone number and if they enjoyed dogsitting.

But when Digger started coming fishing with me and Salt, the perfect fishing dog was born. The myriad stinking things he could find on a small boat probably helped. He would sprawl over the nets, his puppy guts bulging with fish frames, rotten starfish and crab claws. He grew. And grew. He was putting on ten kilos a month. I trained him to sit quietly on the thwart while we played out net and how not to get tangled up in the mesh.

These days, Digger jumps down as the last buoy is thrown into the water and noses around the deck for last week's remnant trumpeters. When it is time to pick up, he leans over the gunwale and watches every fish that comes up. He knows the silver bellies are for him. He thinks we catch all fish just for him. He is so robust in his motivation for food that he sees off anything threatening his feed. Pelicans can make him quite hysterical when they crowd the boat, pulling black bream and mullet out of the net. He's gone over the side after them a few times, dived in headfirst and surfaced like an ungainly seal, spouting brine, circled by smirking birds.

Digger finally grew out of chewing up my furniture and attempting to dismantle the house, not long after my last failed attempt to send him north on the plane. He seems to have finished teething and is evolving from a disaster puppy into a great solid rock of a mastiff mate. But *he's not my dog*.

Recently, his owner flew into town and picked him up for a few days. I arrived home to a strange stillness and keenly felt the absence of that joyful wriggling lump of sea-doggery. 'Welcome home Sarah! I'm so happy you are back! When are we going fishing?' He's made himself indispensable, it seems.

WHILE WE WAITED

The lee of Point Possession, a thermos of coffee, an orange and the talking music of water against the sides of the boat: all these things make the brutal southerly almost bearable. We wait for fish to mesh in nets spread across the sandy bottom where there still lies the remains of another net: made from thick cables to thwart wartime submarine interlopers.

I can hear a two-stroke flogging at top revs and see, way off beyond the wreck of the whale chaser, the speck of another boat.

Salt hears it too. 'Hope they don't run out of fuel before they get wherever they're going.'

We drink some coffee and I smoke a rollie. Salt throws his orange peel into the green water and looks around for the boat. The dinghy doesn't seem to be getting any closer.

'Are they fishermen?'

'Nah,' I say. I can see them now. 'They're both sitting down.' There's only one local commercial fisher who sits at the tiller.

'They're not fishermen anyway. I can hear them talking to each other,' Salt laughs. 'Fishermen know every other bastard can hear them across the water.'

I have to laugh when they finally motor by. Two men singing their hearts into the gathering dusk. Their boat is the size of my twelve-foot Lightburn and, like the *Selkie*, the motor is a brave little six. Full throttle, she is wallowing like a beetle through honey, weighed down to her gunwales by the happy drunken sailors.

'That's just like my *Selkie*!'

'Maybe it *is* your boat.'

For a moment I feed that thought corn-chips and chilli-philly in the scenario-party that is my head. 'Now wouldn't that be fun?'

They cross the channel and head for the abandoned frozen-food factory. Salt and I watch them in mounting consternation.

'They're gonna run into our net!' It's getting dark. I don't want to peel them off the rocks when their prop fouls.

Their motor stops and so does the singing. One man gets up and stumbles to the stern.

'Oh shit.'

'All right.' Salt starts his motor and we head towards them. But just before we get to them, their outboard arcs up again and they continue on to the factory. They pull the little boat up onto the rocks and drag it to their ute. We swing away with a wave and head back to our spot to see out the sunset.

NIGHT OFF

The *Southern Champion* blew a con rod five days out of Mauritius and then laid up at sea for weeks, the crew borrowing each other's DVDs and getting bored out of their brains. They limped into town recently for running repairs and have been setting hearts on fire ever since.

I pedalled my bicycle off to the metropolis to attend an exhibition opening. Trousersnake boys mingled and shared canapés and a brilliant local whisky with the Glamazons. It was a glamorous affair. Lots of great shoes. But this story is more pressing than the international deep-sea fishing trade and the art scene. This is the sordid tale of how I fell off my bicycle that night. Twice.

An artist at the exhibition criticised my new life as a deckie, plundering the ocean's resources for cash. He took a pin to my ballooning ego right when I was being greased up as an ocean-going hero by everyone else – an intrepid fisher-she with a fisherwoman's biceps. I went outside to sit and think quietly about this.

The kind of fishing Salt and I do is small-scale when compared to the toothfish industry. The Patagonian toothfish have been discovered relatively recently in the deepest of Antarctic waters. They can grow to the size and weight of a big man. They are an oily, ice-water fish, so their omega-3 count is obscene. They are probably the ugliest fish you will ever see. And that is about the extent of humanity's knowledge of the

Patagonian toothfish. And the fact that people will pay lots of money for dead ones.

A few years ago, toothfish poachers led the Australian Navy on a merry chase through the Antarctic. The poachers, those age-old chancers with one eye on the horizon, were portrayed in the media as mercenary thieves in their rusting hulk. The Feds' issue with the toothfish poachers was not territory or ethics, but money – serious money. At least that is my take on it. If the Australian Government cared about territory or conservation then perhaps we would see the same action from the navy when the Japanese 'scientists' cruise through the Australian Whale Sanctuary to slaughter minkes.

The fleet of Australian-owned toothfish boats (read Australian, i.e. non-poachers) heads down to the grounds of Heard Island for a bracing three months' hunting. They used to return to Albany for the boat unload, an employment bonanza for strong young men who didn't mind a touch of frostbite hurling one-hundred-kilo fish from one freezer to another. These days the boats unload closer to the market action in Mauritius, Star and Key of the Indian Ocean.

As I justified my own fishing habits to myself, I was snapped out of my reverie by a bunch of sturdy young men, one of whom I'd met a few days earlier. What an assortment – Mauritian, Maori, South African – the United Nations of toothfishermen stood before me.

'Hey Sarah! Do you know where we can get some ... you know, some hootie?'

(I thought: it's the curly hair that makes me look like a shaggy stoner. That's why I get asked this all the time. Hang on, he said 'hootie' not 'hooch'. What the hell? O-oh. Ewwg!)

'I'm kind of out of the loop with that sort of thing,' I explained apologetically. Why was this nice young man asking me to pimp for him? I got all flustered. His Mauritian mate smiled at me with carnivorous intent and took my photo with his mobile phone.

Mr Mauritius took another couple of hours (roughly till closing time) to decide he was definitely following me home. There was no changing his mind. He was on a quest all of his own idea to uncover the sensual gifts of a true Albanian. He would not consider 'fuck off' as a reasonable obstacle. Unfortunately for him, at that stage of the night, he was dealing with Sarah the Warrior Princess and she possessed a bicycle.

I fled into the deep, dark night. He was fleet of foot but I was so much fleeter by wheel. I could hear his footsteps thudding behind me and his throaty, anguished cry, 'Sarah, Sarah!' I rode that bicycle like a demon. My heart thumped with whisky and hubris. Took the corner at the town hall and gunned it home.

Well. Sounds good. I took the corner and gunned it, like, I ramped the throttle on an iron charger throbbing between my thighs and performed an attention-seeking rumble-streak down the highway. The truth is, I came to grief quietly and in slow motion when I hit the curb outside the kindergarten.

The whole Christmas party crashed with me; a half-empty bottle of wine (not half-full by this point), my handbag, mobile phone and my beautiful grey coat, which I still haven't found. (If you have found it, please give it back. You will never be able to wear it in this town and anyway, it's itchy.)

My body hurt a bit but my whiskyed adrenalin helped me out of the gutter and I rose to travel the road once more. I'd forgotten all about my bereft toothfisherman and was alternately giggling and nursing a rapidly swelling elbow. If you fall off, then you gotta get back on again, was my reasoning. Yes?

The second crash really hurt.

OH, 'TIS MY DELIGHT, ON A SHINY NIGHT …

Salt thought he would give me training in some more nefarious activities. In the middle of the night, he took the boat straight to the buoy roped to a skeletal, submerged tree. Silken clouds strained the frugal moonlight across the water.

'No lights. No talking – voices carry across the water,' the ancient mariner growled at me. The net, with extra-heavy lead line, was sunk below the surface. An hour later we pulled up fat black bream that gleamed golden like dollars in the murky waters, eight inches apart. We hauled in that net in fifteen minutes flat, dumping it fish and all onto a hasty tarp, leaving the unmeshing till later.

Salt was jollier than I've ever seen him. He was back on the game, faithful to his ancestral roots and he belted out 'The Lincolnshire Poacher', forgetting all about his own earlier cautions.

When I was bound apprentice in famous Lincolnshire
'Twas well I served my master for nigh on seven years
Till I took up poaching, as you shall quickly hear
Oh, 'tis my delight, on a shiny night
In the season of the year.

As me and my companions was setting out a snare
'Twas then we spied the gamekeeper, for him we didn't care.
For we can wrestle and fight, my boys, and jump from anywhere.
Oh, 'tis my delight, on a shiny night
In the season of the year.

Over water darkened by paperbarks lining the banks, I handled the boat and was guided back to shore by Salt's gravelly rhyme and song, the decks smelling of clean, fresh river fish. Well, he's trolleyed, I thought. He's been drinking cask wine. We'll be bush-bashing for hours to find our camp again. How will he find our launching spot in this melancholy maze of strange groves and rivulets? Every landing looked the same to me in the sulky midnight gloom.

He guided me straight to the tree that my elastic-sided boots lay beneath. I pulled the boots onto my bare feet and then backed the four-wheel drive down to the water in the dark. Salt, that canny old sea-dog, had just presented me another tutorial on the practical theory on one of the finer arts – and how fine it is only the initiated know.

NO JOB FOR A SOBER MAN

'The best place to be,' said Salt. 'No slinking around the paperbarks tonight. Right here, where everyone can see us.'

The last time we visited, we had the place to ourselves. Now, the moment we crunched on to the little beach, people were everywhere and especially interested in us, it seemed. I hoped Salt knew his stuff.

I chucked the swags out of the boat and they bounced on the coarse yellow sand. A late afternoon sun considered the horizon. Salt backed the trailer into the inlet. I rolled up my jeans, exposing lurid tattoos, and stepped into the water to bounce the little boat off her trailer. I could feel the air that the gathering mob sucked in. We held our breath too, hoping the silver paint would not scrape off the boat to expose the licence numbers to militant anglers.

There was a pair of Irish newlyweds. She had hair like nasturtiums in the setting sun, red dress against silver water and she posed for her photographer husband. An old couple from Queensland cleaned black bream near where my swag lay and threw the guts to pelicans. And here also, came he: civic policeman, citizen sheriff. His rotund, red-faced stance said it all: mouse wife, lapdog mate; a man otherwise rendered impotent by his own retirement. He stopped to check the Queenslanders' bucket and then made his way to us, his friend following him.

'You after mullet, mate? You'll need some net, y'know. Got some net?'

'I dunno. I thought we'd go lookin' for a coupla bream.' Salt was all innocent tourist. He didn't want anyone to see those nets stashed under tarps in the boat.

'There's plenty around.'

'Are they nice to eat?' I asked.

'Oh, we catch and release normally,' Civic Cop shrugged. 'But they're all right. If you like fish.'

Salt was extraordinary. He just smiled and nodded. I remembered his rants about both self-appointed sheriffs *and* catch-and-release advocates. ('Just torture a fish for an hour like a cat with a mouse and then let it go without eatin' it. You'd get arrested if you tried that with a cow or a sheep. Blimmin' cruel. Eat it, or leave it alone, I reckon.')

'I hope you're not going to smoke onboard, girly.' Civic Cop nodded towards Salt, as I rolled a durry. 'What would the boss have to say about you smoking around all those petrol fumes?'

'He's just not that fussed, *mate*.'

We all watched two men in a tinny picking up nets close to shore. They threw out undersized bream. Pelicans tumoured around the boat.

'You using net?'

Salt played deaf, not a hard ask. 'Don't forget the bait!' he shouted at me and threw a tangled mess of gummed up fishing rods into the boat. I climbed into the dinghy to tidy things. The two fishers finished stowing their nets and motored into the beach. Civic Cop's focus on us began to waver. He strode over to seagull the two fishers' catch, his mate following behind. He called back to me, 'Now don't go over the bag limit, will ya.'

I don't know how much more of this story I can tell, before I would have to kill you. It was a sweaty night. An apprenticeship with Salt can be precarious at best. Salt's take on the night's work, as we drove out of the paperbarks at three in the morning with no headlights, was, 'Well thank fuck for that. Every flap of a bream's tail was too much racket. Get me some plonk next time, deckie. That was no job for a sober man.'

BAIE DE DEUX PEUPLES

Salt dropped me onto a quiet beach heaped with bleached ribbon weed at the west end of Two Peoples Bay. Those soft dry beds of weed looked so inviting, the perfect place to kip – but I knew that Tiger Snake Swamp lay matted below the strands of tea-tree just metres away, and oblivion among those critters, even on this warm eve, was not a thought to entertain for long.

It is here that the granite gently slopes down into the water. The bay whalers of old knew it was a perfect place to winch up the huge carcasses of the humpbacks and flense them of their blubber by peeling it away like mango skin.

Now there is no blood. When it's dark and the moon has died, stars streak silver on the skin of the sea and I've heard the breathing and singing of whales all around me. Once I tracked them through the water by their ghostly wake of phosphorescence.

This night, Venus shone red with the vanquished sun. Gleaming silver sickles of King George whiting came up in the nets in clumps of three or four, ten dollar notes, to become subjects of queue-inducing hysteria down at the Sunday markets.

The onshore wind pushing us into the surf, the wet jeans that stiffen into stovepipes, bare toes on a cold steel deck – all of those things are worth a catch like this.

A giant stingray followed us along the net, his bat sails undulating against the green of water over a white, sandy bottom. Squid flew away like wraiths as we hauled up the net and shot sooty plumes of ink, hovering just out of the fluorescent light to watch us pull up a whiting with a perfect crescent chomped out of its head. Squid must love that rush of blood. An oily little shark, its tail and dorsal fin slicing, meandered by, hunting.

We sat for an unusually long time in the boat after we'd finished with the fish and the nets, faces parallel with the stars and the nippled mountain looming against a dark sky to the east. When we finally landed, Salt trudged up the beach to get the car. I stood in the shallows and waited for the shock of red tail-lights in the night, for the rumbling of the four-wheel drive reversing across hard sand and into the water. I played the little boat against her ragged rope.

BEACH SEINING FOR
GARDIES AT PEACEFUL BAY

A chill wind blew off the sea. Salt and I pulled the garfish seine net onto the little rowboat. The wind crept through my woollies and the sand in the nets blew into my eyes. I finished loading with my sunglasses on in the half-dark. Then I lost the bung. Then Salt lost the padlock key to the towbar – in the same patch of grass as the invisible bung.

I was thinking: everything's going bad. Oh well. There's been shit shots before and there will again. The last bad one, the net found a submerged rock and couldn't stay away from it.

We went inside the shack and made a cup of tea, waited for the night to come on.

Around the corner from Foul Bay at Peaceful Bay, the wind died. It felt almost warm. Salt backed the trailer down to the water. We launched the boat and pushed her out. He rowed off into the night, with me standing on shore holding the end of the seine net.

A beautiful night, glassed off with green harbour markers flashing and bobbing in the water. I lost sight of Salt and then saw him again as he pulled the boat into shore about two hundred metres along the beach and stumbled overboard. By the time he'd anchored the dinghy, I'd nearly walked my end of the net to where the truck was parked. Every so often, I'd shine the torch across the water to find the white buoy marking the centre purse of the net.

'Start pullin' that lead line in!'
'Keep pullin' that lead line in!'

'Get that lead line in. Get that pocket happening!'

Running up and down the shoreline to grab more floats and pulling the seine net in from the sea brought up a sweat. Salt just ambled along until he was near the truck too and then we both pulled the thrashing pocket of fish into the lacy water's edge.

A huge stingray floundered, all elegance lost against the net and the sand. He was swiftly flipped out and he slid into the sea. I kept a weather eye out for the eel tails of cobbler. Blowies began rolling about in the ebb like spiky footballs. I could smell the garfish. Whiting, gardies, herring, all shining and writhing in the torchlight.

A beautiful night.

SHIT SHOT

Two more lessons for the apprenticeship – bad seine shots always happen to fisherfolk when they are down to their last fifty cents but tend to be a good thing when other fisherfolk are watching. To illustrate the first lesson, Bullet was at Irwin's the same week that all his fishing licences, land rates and vehicle registration bills came in. While Salt and I hauled in boxes of yellowfin and King George whiting, he set the same size nets across much the same grounds and got bugger all. Fishing can be fickle and charmless like that.

With seining, we see the fish swim into the bay: the dark stain of tons of salmon, or the fins of sea mullet splashing and writhing on the water's skin, or the smelly glitter of gardies in torchlight. Whenever there are other fishers around, there is a sudden rush of gnarly men to get the boat loaded with net and down to the water. You'd never believe men like that could run so fast. They push the little dinghy into the sea, the rower spools the net behind them and rows in a big arc, back to the beach. Then they pull both ends of the net in.

The last bad shot was at the salmon camp. The sun was setting and the wind farm made asterisks over the cliffs across the bay. A ute full of blokes got bogged on the beach below the camp. Actually they weren't bogged but suspended by the car's engine block on a large piece of granite. They were all drinking and I doubt they saw the rock in the half-light.

For some reason Salt and I were cranky with each other, or just plain cranky. Anyway we weren't talking much as we loaded the gardie net onto the dinghy. Loading a seine net is an art. Later it's got to play out nice and smooth, straight off the stern of the boat. The pocket in the middle has to be folded just right, so it opens out on its own.

The men in the ute were supposed to be shipping out on the sharker anchored by the island but had forgotten to buy ice. All the factories had shut for the day but the bottle shops hadn't and so I think they settled down to drinking instead. I know their skipper Philthy. He's got a PhD in bugs or something. He quotes Jorge Luis Borges' 'The Library of Babel' at me when he's drunk. Philthy is a fidgety bantam with a brain like a computer but one day he saw the light and realised he didn't want to be a scientist. He wanted to be a fisherman.

One of his deckies looked like he'd come straight from the darkened back rooms of Darwin's Vic Hotel. Tattooed legs, stubbies, a flannel shirt and a fragile nature, he was a man pushed out of polite society and therefore welcomed by Philthy's operation. No social worker but a man with a philanthropic heart, Philthy has been known to throw those hankering sorts overboard but only when the boat makes it to swimming distance of an island.

I had gone to school with the second deckie. He was blond, a long-haired roughie back then. He hasn't changed a bit. His father was a fisherman too.

The third deckie was from Carnarvon. His diamond-shaped head prickled with a buzz cut the whole way around. He must have been in his twenties but he had the hard face of a man who'd spent a lot of time in the desert. He shot dingoes for a living but while the floods covered the North-West he was on sabbatical, until the earth dried up again.

When it was dark enough Salt drove the boat down to the beach. I walked and the deckies followed in a ragtag, shambling mob. Salt was pissed off. He hates other fishermen watching him work.

I pushed out the boat, with Salt at the oars. There is a rock about fifty metres from shore and I always have to walk the net over this rock so we don't get snagged up. This night a weird swell washed in. Salt rowed out, with me holding the end of the seine net. The waves kept pulling the net back onto the rock.

Darwin started up a strange dance on the foaming edges of the water. He capered through the swell, holding up his chequered shirt, the waves splashing the tattoos on his legs.

'He's lookin' for pipis,' the dogger told me. 'With his toes. He's been going on about the bloody cockles for days now. It's all he wanted to do when he got down south.'

The wind came up and competed with Philthy's rendition of hexagonal vortexes of infinite libraries. I felt the net grab at the rock again and managed to unhook it, briefly. Then Salt was shouting at me from up the beach. He'd already anchored the boat in the sand and was working his way along the end of the net.

'I'm snagged!' I yelled back.

Salt stumped along the beach, grabbed the rope off me, tugged it. He started into the water. He swam out to the rock in his clothes and ripped the net away. Then he stamped back to the boat and his end of the net.

We hauled.

Three herring.

We all looked at those three fish flapping on the torchlit sand.

Then Philthy and his deckies rocked their four-wheel drive off the offending stone with a nasty crunching sound and took off down the beach looking for salmon, spraying bright plumes of burning cigarette butts and beer cans in their wake.

Salt and I looked at each other. We were both soaked and encrusted with fine white beach sand.

'Just as well they didn't see us catch any fish,' he muttered at me. 'Those bastards would tell *everyone*.'

DOGS OF THE SEA
AND OTHER ANIMALS

The dog leans over the bow and his whole body tenses as he captures the dolphin's breath in his nostrils. He knows they are mammals from their smell. The dolphins roll over and watch him ... 'Come in and play!' They tease him and I can see that Digger would be with them in a second if he knew he could fly through the sea like those sea-dogs. His frustration is palpable.

The smirking seal running along our nets, night-time visitations from humpback whales, feeding wobbegongs and wanting to live in the belly of an elephant: interactions with south coast sea mammals and other big critters are fragmentary moments when the rest of the world falls away.

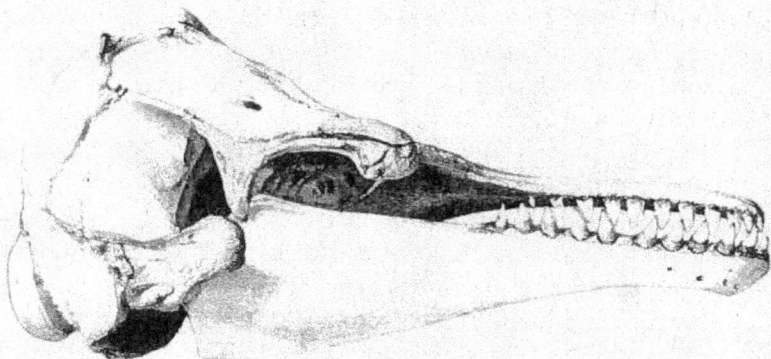

W Wing del et lith.   Hullmandel & Walton Lithographers

ORCA INTERMEDIA.

FINGER FOOD

Twertawaning is the Noongar name for the 'old/past dogs' according to linguist C.G. Brandenstein – dolphins who worked with the people.

A Noongar elder of Albany told the story of the 'clever man' who stood on the beach with his sticks, tapping them and singing, calling in the dolphins. Fires burned along the white sands of the bay. The dolphins herded the salmon into the shallows. Lean men waded into the water and speared the salmon. Sometimes they could just pick them up off the sand. It is a bloody deal, worked out between man and dolphin over millennia. The dolphins are still doing it. An old fisherman told me that one year the dolphins herded a hundred ton of salmon into the pool at Nanarup and kept them there for days, feasting on the pilchards that the salmon had thrown up.

This day the dogs of the sea hunted and played in our wake and bow wave. Their white shadows flew through the sea and they turned up their faces to see us. Drowned pirates, frightened by the magic of their captive Dionysus, they are repentant and will do all they can to help sailors.

We were not to be shipwrecked this day but I nearly lost all four fingers from one hand. We trolled for salmon with thick line and a silver lure with barbarous hooks. Shearwaters, gannets, ospreys and Pacific gulls wheeled all around us. Pilchards skipped off the water, chased to the surface by salmon and bonito. Birds worked all over the Sound.

I lost a salmon. They were too overfed to take my lure seriously. I stood on deck, the odd slop that rocks between the islands making me unsteady. Salmon line wrapped around my fingers. I threw out the lure again.

Salt gunned the motor.

Line around my fingers and line around the propeller.

Just like that.

But it broke! The line actually broke!

The engine sounded clunky. I told Salt about the prop and climbed over the stern to untangle the fishing line. My hand hurt in the cold water but there was much to do.

About twenty minutes later I examined the deep, burning scores across all four fingers of my right hand. As soon as I considered my potential for fingerlessness I became wobbly and suddenly, I just really wanted to go home, to leave the Sound to the fish, the gannets and the dogs of the sea.

MAN BITES SHARK BITES DOG

A humpback whale leapt about by the first portside marker outside the channel. We were setting flathead nets at dusk when I saw his body shooting out of the sea like black ink, the plumes of white spray on his return. His tail made a perfect crescent against the reddening sky. We motored into the Sound later to look for him but he was long gone. There was not even a footprint, those flat, circular marks on the water caused by the massive displacement of water from the thrust of a whale's tail.

I saw a stingray in the shallows too that afternoon. It was as big as the rug in my living room. Its body was patterned with white paisley marks against black skin. I'd know that stingray anywhere if I ever saw it again.

The next morning, we pulled up the harbour nets to find a smaller stingray with its stinger bitten clean off and its body sliced open with little bleeding arcs. Sharper than any filleting knife were the attacker's teeth. Salmon trout lined up in the net with only their heads left.

'Bronzy,' said Salt.

Salt is always teaching me to identify predators. Sometimes the crab pots are full of carapaces and chewed-up claws, when an octopus has got in. Leatherjackets eat crabs too. In the harbour nets, crabs tangle in the mesh where they have gone in after the herring or bream. If there are crabs in the net, then the gummy sharks might follow them into the mesh. Sometimes the flathead nets come up with row upon row of heads or mangled carcasses with only their livers missing.

That's the seal.

There has been a five-metre white pointer hanging around in the Sound recently. It's had a go at a few boat propellers and gone along the fisherman Grievous' squid lines, stealing the bait, jigs and all. *Five metres.* My friends who kayak on Sundays have been sticking to the harbour.

Snow said he saw the shark circling Seal Rock. You can see Seal Rock from the lookout on Marine Drive. It's a rounded granite rock where the old bull seal hangs out, his harem lolling around him in the surging swell. Snow said this shark circled the rock for an age, hungry-like, round and round that big round rock, waiting for the old man seal to make *just one* mistake.

Whether the seals have been attacked or just frightened out of the Sound, they have been leaving the flathead nets alone. Salt reckons it's a good thing sharks like the white pointers are protected, especially when they do such a good job of keeping the seals away from 'his' flathead.

They weren't always protected. When I was about eight, my dad came home from the fish factory and said he wanted to show me something. We got into the Kingswood. He drove back to the factory and walked me over to the freezer rooms. 'Come and have a look at this.'

The freezer was the size of a small hall, with racks against the walls full of salmon or sardines or whatever was running at the time. My shoes stuck to the frozen floor. I saw the shark, frozen solid and lying upon carpenter trestles right in the centre of the room, like an exhibit. Its skin was black. It was the most beautiful creature I had ever seen.

Dad said, 'See if you can touch both eyes at once.'

I couldn't. When I stretched my arms across the head of the monster, I couldn't touch both its eyes. He said then that the same fisherman had caught another great white a few weeks before, and that when he cut it open he found pieces of a kid's tricycle and half a dog inside its stomach.

It all just seems to go around and around. Perhaps the big sharks were coming in again because they were hungry and after seal. The seals consider our nets a bonanza, as much as the leatheries and the octopus enjoy the crab pots.

As a newcomer, I know it's their patch I am working and I don't mind the seal or other critters eating some of the catch. Salt doesn't agree. They are *his* waters, he reckons, as much as the next seal, stingray or shark. Perhaps he can claim resident predator status, having worked these waters for near on sixty years.

SEAL MEDLEY

'We'll have to get you a gun, girl,' Salt grinned at me, knowing my response. 'Just like Annie Oakley, except you'll be sorting out seals. What's the matter ... don't you like guns?'

I'm fine with guns. He knows I was raised by folk with an affinity for black powder.

'Ahh, shit. Don't tell me. *You like seals*, don't you?'

Last night as we hauled, a seal fought us for the net. It ate every fish, working its way from the red buoy at the channel entrance to the boat. The fish it could not tear out, it bit in half, ate their livers and devoured their roe-rich bellies. Finally it arrived at the boat and I peered down into the water to see its phosphorescent gleam undulating around the net. Like a marauding wraith, this seal.

In May, I camped on Breaksea Island. Every morning I lay across lichen and stone to watch the seals and sea lions. They rolled in the briny and ambulated into sheltered coves using their flippers as sails. On a high rock the babies gathered in their creche. The seals' capacity for pleasure was heartening for me, having escaped to the island for some peace and quiet. I needed no further evidence that lying around on warm rocks is good for the soul.

From the highest point of Breaksea Island where giant, streaked megaliths swooped down to the water on an angle that made my feet tingle, I saw a seal swimming far below. Smooth, missile-like; not the delightful, doe-eyed darlings I'd seen earlier, this seal was hunting and its speed indicated a carnivorous intent.

One afternoon on the island I went hunting for limpets along the rocks for bait. A curious female sprouted out of the sea beside me, blowing a mist of air and brine, eyeing me. She dived and surfaced again through her footprint. I sang to her, as loud and true as I could. She snorted, dived and returned to watch me. For a moment I saw myself reflected in her huge, black eyes – standing on the rocks in a bright red jacket, wielding a filleting knife and singing.

When the resident seal was slaughtered at Emu Point a few years ago, older locals who could speculate on such matters looked to Salt. He didn't kill that seal. He did write a letter to the local newspaper, saying that tourist operators shouldn't feed wildlife for their own monetary gain, claiming it provoked bad behaviour in animals and humans alike.

But the reason for the sudden interest in Salt after the death of Sammy the Seal had nothing to do with the letter. A decade earlier Salt had created a furore by offering a reward to anyone who could 'deal with' a rogue bull seal that had been raiding nets. 'I didn't kill that seal either,' Salt told me. 'But someone did something.' I suspect that Salt was quite happy to wear it at the time. The resulting drama made him more salty and notorious than ever and someone had seen to the seal.

He told me a story then, about the killing of a seal sixty years ago. 'The old man and me went out to Waychinicup. He was gonna set some nets and catch some skippy, and right there, lying on the rocks in front of him was this big old bull seal. The old man picked up his axe and walked over there and put that axe right through his skull.'

I must have looked horrified. 'Why?'

'He'd driven the truck fifty miles to set nets. Five kids to feed and all that fuel and he knew the seal would eat every fucking fish before he got them out of the mesh.' Salt shrugged. 'Just the way it was, back then.'

WAITING FOR BARDOT

'You gone to see Captain Crackpot yet?' Salt asked me.

'Who?'

'Isn't he coming to town to save the whales?'

Ahh. The Captain and his *Sea Shepherd* mob.

Apparently the *Steve Irwin* and the *Brigitte Bardot* were coming into port to launch their season's campaign from the old whaling station. The dramas continue to play out in our town, the last land-based whaling station in the southern hemisphere.

'I think he's an arsehole,' Salt was trying to get a rise out of me. 'Putting people out of work. He should get a real job instead of sailing around the world, stopping good people from doing theirs.'

The problem with working in a small boat is that you are stuck with whatever conversation is going on. Sometimes when Salt wants a barney, I'll ask him to drop me off on an island. That is a good lurk. This afternoon I was forced to stay aboard and, well, I'm quite partial to a rant if it suits me.

'Where was the Australian Navy when the whalers were cruising through the Australian Whale Sanctuary? Where? 'Crackpot' Watson was the only one out there. It's a territorial matter as much as anything but the government were behaving like total limpdicks.' (I've been trying really hard to rein in my deckie mouth but, at sea, things are different.)

'I reckon the Australian Government has some agreement with the Japanese we don't know about,' Salt said. 'But they've been eating whale meat for centuries. That should be their right. Imagine how many people you could feed with a single whale.'

'Poor people?'

'Yeah.'

'They can't afford to eat Japanese whale meat.'

He muttered something about poor people breeding too much and I smiled away to the water. I know he hates that.

'But they should be able to kill whales if it is a part of their ancestral heritage,' said Salt.

'Yeah, with diesel-powered gunships, thousands of nautical miles from their own waters. Yeah.'

Salt laid both the oars across the gunwales to make a seat for himself. 'When I was whaling here in the '60s, oh, it was a good life. We were a bunch of rascals, out at sea, coming in with shitloads of money, tearing up the town ... yeah, it was good. But I wouldn't do it now. I never liked seeing those creatures die. It was a terrible thing, to see them die.'

ARCHIVAL SONGSTERS OF PELAGIA

Picture this: you are driving around aimlessly on a Sunday, looking for something to look at. As you do the curve on Marine Drive you see a whole bunch of people standing together, quite a gathering. When you pull up to see what is happening, you discover a truly disconcerting combination of citizens. The pock-nosed real estate salesman is holding hands with the Noongar elder. Night nurses yawn and rub their careworn paws against the Health Minister's Chanel jacket. A couple of teenage girls actually smile at their mothers and the mothers actually smile back, before looking out to sea.

All right, I'm making that last bit up. But whales *do* these things to people.

When whales appear, rolling off their barnacles on the white sandy bottom of Middleton Beach and parading their babies, people who would normally stride past each other actually begin to commune. They lend out binoculars and stand close enough to feel the warmth coming off each other's bodies. Everyone seems to know that the whales are here to visit us.

Salt, the old whaler, came back from a trip in the Sound, all misty-eyed and converted.

'It was great,' he said. 'They swam right under the tinny and all around us. We could have touched them.' He said it was the closest he'd been to a whale 'in peacetime'.

Native American tradition says that whales are the record keepers of the earth. These pelagic archivists, closer to us in physical structure and sentience than their fishy fellows, are said to have witnessed times when the earth went through catastrophic change. They were land-based creatures when the oceans of the world rose and their motherland Mu sank beneath the waters forever.

I think that when we see the whales, something in us recognises them as our archivists. They remember where we came from. With such memory, it is no wonder that the people of Albany are in love with whales, are now humbled by the leviathans gracing us with their presence. It is only thirty-odd years ago that the last whale was harpooned in Albany waters.

MOUNTAIN MAN, THE FUGITIVE AND THE WHALES

'Pick up any hitchhikers lately?' Salt asked me when I arrived at the inlet. It didn't help that Nick Cave's *Murder Ballads* had been on repeat for the long drive. I'd passed three police cars on the highway and that made the road unusual and slightly fraught. The Bad Seeds carrying on about general human nastiness only made me jumpier. Salt told me then that a fugitive was on the loose in these parts. Apparently, he'd escaped police custody in a town near the inlet and had taken to the bush. They'd put out the planes and dogs after him. 'He's without his meds,' Salt said, looking at me meaningfully. 'Better keep the cars locked.'

To make things more interesting, Mountain Man had moved back to his perch right next to the only toilet in the isolated fishing camp. His set-up of a ute and trailer would be sweet if he didn't swathe the whole circus in a shambolic mess of white canvas. At first I thought he was drying out his annexe but it was sunny for days. His camp shone white through the trees from every angle on the point. But my main beef was that he was a shouter and he completely freaked me out.

Last time he camped here, he shouted at me at five thirty in the morning when I was bumbling up to the loo. I got yelled at to 'go and live in the Tanami if you want to wander about with your fucking dog'. I thought then that *he'd* be better off in the Tanami Desert, or as far away from me as possible, or least a bit further away from the only public toilet in a fifty-kilometre radius, if he really wanted to do a Greta Garbo.

So this time around after we set nets in the evening, I sat on the toilet and could not persuade any of my bodily functions to function. Why? Because it was getting dark and I cannot leisurely eliminate when someone is yelling next to the corrugated iron wall, 'Told you not to put yer fuckin' nose in there you shit of a thing put yer nose in the fly net mosquito net if you put yer fuckin' nose in there again I'm gonna get fuckin' mosquitos biting me and I'm gonna fuckin' flog yer you hear that I'll fuckin' hit yer I'm sick of it.'

I rarely see Mountain Man. Even when he yells at me, he keeps out of sight. I may see his thin neck and his head crowned with a colourless beanie peering at me from the windows of his car, or I may see a wisp of smoke from his camp fire behind his car, or the pointed ears of his long-suffering, yellow-eyed cur dog.

I sat on the toilet with no door, completely unable to shit whilst Mountain Man continued his rant.

I studied the signs written in black Artline on the toilet wall.

PUT THE LID DOWN.

DID YOU SHUT THE LID? NO? OH NO NO!

(It's a complete failure of a compost dunny and is filling up at a rather alarming rate.) I gave up. He was still shouting. I watched for his shadow in the doorway, saw it was clear and walked out, avoiding looking towards his camp. Don't make eye contact. Don't make eye contact.

Then I realised I'd forgotten to shut the lid.

Back at our fire, I said to Unruly and Salt, 'I think I'd prefer to die of faecal impaction before I use that dunny again.'

Salt snorted, 'Yeah, it's fillin' up, girl.'

'No, it's Mountain Man, he scares the crap out of me. Well, actually my crap's too scared to come out while he's yellin' at me.'

'He's yellin' at his dog,' said Unruly.

'Oh. Well. He's creepy.'

'He's pretty harmless,' said Unruly kindly. 'Just took too many trips when he was young. Lives around all these beaches, he does. He was at Bremer last week. Or maybe Normans. He won't hurt ya.'

Salt and I both locked our cars that night. When I unzipped my tent, I shone the torch around before I stepped inside. In the morning I was climbing into my wet-weather gear, struggling to fit the plastic pants over my boots, when a silvery four-wheel drive cruised past all kinda sharky, no lights in the gloom before the sun. They drove onto the beach, turned around and went past our camp again. Plain clothes, looking for an escapee, I thought. Maybe. No doubt. Cops.

An early nor'-westerly struck up a tune on the water while I picked undersized crabs from the net and shook out the coral. Salt backed along the net into the wind, keeping the propeller off the cork lines. He tried cracking a few jokes but they weren't really working on me.

I dug a bush toilet for myself in a nice quiet *non-shouting* space. Later, while I was packing the bream into boxes and icing them down, the radio announcer said that they still hadn't caught the fugitive. He repeated that the man didn't have his medication.

At the roadhouse, fifty kilometres away, I bought some fuel for the boat and the woman at the counter volunteered an A4 printout of the runaway prisoner. He didn't look like the fugitive from *Great Expectations*. He wasn't whiskered and gnarly with bad teeth and nasty eyes and a pocked nose. He was a nice-looking young man, slim, pleasant, even given the police ID board he held in front of his chest – from different police station to the one where cops had botched his latest arrest.

'But apparently his hair is shorter now,' she said. 'And he's wearing shorts and a t-shirt.'

We were both quiet for a moment and then she said, 'Poor bugger. I hope he's okay. It was really cold last night.'

On examining the picture, he definitely wasn't Mountain Man but that wasn't much of a relief because it meant there were two freaked-out folk wandering around. The inlet is a good place to slide like a needle into the veins of country and never be seen again ... except by people like us living there.

Before dawn the next day, I lay in my tent listening to the swans and the ducks and the grebes awaking. Then there was a new sound ...

A trumpeting, a *blow* like someone breathing through an amplified didgeridoo, then the slapping of huge wads of flesh and skin against the skin of the sea.

The whales. *The whales are back.*

Salt put the kettle on and turned up the radio. The fugitive had handed himself into a farmer last night. He'd been taken to hospital with hypothermia. Mountain Man had finally quit his hollering too. He walked past the camp with his dog and threw out a tattered sleeve in what I realised later was a wave hello.

The whales. I could hear them from where I stood drinking my coffee, looking out to the sandbar. I couldn't see them but the chilled dawn air was so still that I heard them like they were right in front of me. They sang for hours that morning. Ten or fifteen whales, singing the story of their return from Antarctica.

BREATHING AWAY THE MACHINE

An old lady told me once that her people used to take their teenage girls to Waychinicup for healing, to fix them up when they got sick or sad. This place has a kind of fey wildness that never fails to infect people with a creeping sense that strange, shy creatures are watching from the breathing scrub and waters. Waychinicup feels like it is making me better.

A river runs through the deep, moist valley, darkening with the tannins of tea-tree until it reaches the stone-bound inlet. The sea squeezes in through granite gatekeepers and the two surges of river and sea combine to make a gentle, breathing tide.

We returned to Waychinicup last night, swept down into the primal contours of her gully. I feel elation on return to this country – that, and a curious sense of unbelonging. That last drive down to sea level, the water laid out like silver paper between creased hills, makes me feel all of these things. I brought the girl Pearlie with me and set up the tent for her, watched her burrow into a swag and sleep. She slept for fourteen hours.

'I want to live there,' I pointed out the granite elephant to Salt, the lithic, slumbering creature, one of the many strange rock formations that bind the inlet. Perfect hindquarters displayed her fanny to the world. Someone had lovingly constructed a dry stone wall around her hind legs, to keep out the wind. Inside was the carcass of a cooking fire.

'I want to live in the belly of that elephant.'

'Well, the rent would be cheap.'

We both said, 'Till the ranger drops in.'

The mountain above is sprayed with rocks, streaked with rain. In a not so distant past, a pilot, legendary spotter of whale chasing days, along with some detectives on a search for floating drums of illegal drugs, obliterated themselves and their plane against this unforgiving mountain.

I could live here though, away from the complications of machinations of my current existence. I could fish for just enough to eat each day and garnish that with native spinach and celery. I could grow quiet and hermity, surprise myself with words occasionally. I could live in the belly of the elephant. And I would sing. I would watch and listen to the gentle meanderings of this isolated universe. I would stitch myself into the inlet. I could do that.

Till the ranger dropped in.

WAY, WAY WAYCHINICUP

An old man wobbegong slides back into his stony grotto.

We wrestle a whole school of clumsy, striped ludericks out of the nets and slip them back into the water.

A Port Jackson shark, a dinosaur, the biggest I've ever seen, fins like Cessna wings, crusher teeth hooked into the mono. I untangle him, eyeing his dorsal spike. He folds back into the murk and just ... disappears.

Glossy skipjack the size of my forearm. Keepers.

Poisonous angelfish, their bristling spikes keep them entangled.

Cobbler. Waddy thump.

Black branches of long-sodden tea-trees, dreamcatchered with green ribbon grass.

Oily, soft yelloweye mullet

Good honest herring.

And a quickening pace to the buoy.

When the sun came up I filleted the skippy. The wobbegong had taken a bite from each one. I threw the frames back into his grotto, shooing away the Pacific gulls.

'You feeding that bloody carpety again?' yelled Salt from the shore. 'All the better, so I can catch him later and *eat* the fat bastard!'

WHALE TRACKS

Tonight the humpbacks visited. We were waiting for whiting to mesh, sitting out the sunset, twitchy with the need to pick up the nets and see what was there and not leave it too long before the dastardly squid ate the lot.

Sometimes the waiting becomes the event and the nets are a mere by-product. Tonight was like that. The sun set over the houses and dunes at Goode Beach and at an indefinable moment of half-light, the motorbike frogs began revving from their swamp behind the primary dune. A couple fishing on the beach turned on their gas lamp. Mares' tails and mackerel scales, a sure sign of storms to come, dotted and streaked the sky with crazy colour. Out to sea, Breaksea Island glowed magenta and white-water monsters crashed against her rocks.

Three humpback whales rounded Mistaken Island. Two of them cruised back out of the bay as I cut the motor. The third stayed nearby. I watched his footprints slowly dot across the surface as he moved towards us.

The footprints enchanted me: the closeness of this beast, his massive bulk beneath the surface, undetectable but for those circles of calm.

He rose to the surface about fifty metres from the boat, presented a mottled fin and rolled sideways to look at us. His head was all bumpy and alien, cowled with barnacles and glistening with brine. He breathed in the night and then arched straight into a dive.

'That means he's diving deep,' Salt told me. 'The way he arched sharp like that. He won't come up for a while.'

We began looking around for footprints. I was reminded of sitting in a paddock, giving up on catching an errant horse. Eventually the horse would eat its way in a spiral to my feet.

And there he was! About ten metres from the boat. We both stood in the *very little tinny*.

'Jeez,' said Salt. 'I hope he doesn't have any barnacles he wants rubbing off.'

The whale dived again, then a footprint appeared right beside the boat. I spun around, trying to track the whale and turned the wrong way. Finally, turning clockwise instead of withershins, I saw it. A perfect clock face of whale tracks. Salt and I stood in the centre like the hour and minute hands.

When we saw the whale again, he was heading out into the open water, spouted and then arched into another deep, long dive.

'Well,' said I.

The water lay completely still, glassed off, the sun nearly set and everything silent but for those frogs. We stood in the dinghy in a perfect circle of whale tracks.

'This is really quite unpleasant,' said Salt. 'I can think of better places to be, like sitting on my couch at home, watching TV or something.'

HOW TO EAT FISH

'How to Eat Fish' is about more than recipes, though there is more than one way to cook a fish and a few of them are mentioned here. 'How to Eat Fish' is a less-than-formal foray into the politics of sustainable seafood in the south-west fishery. It's interesting that the fish highest in the 'good oil' and lowest in heavy metals are often the more sustainable run fish such as herring, mullet and salmon. Run fish are also cheaper and most likely to be sold for bait or pet food, while the Australian market tends to hunger for less sustainable or even imported seafood.

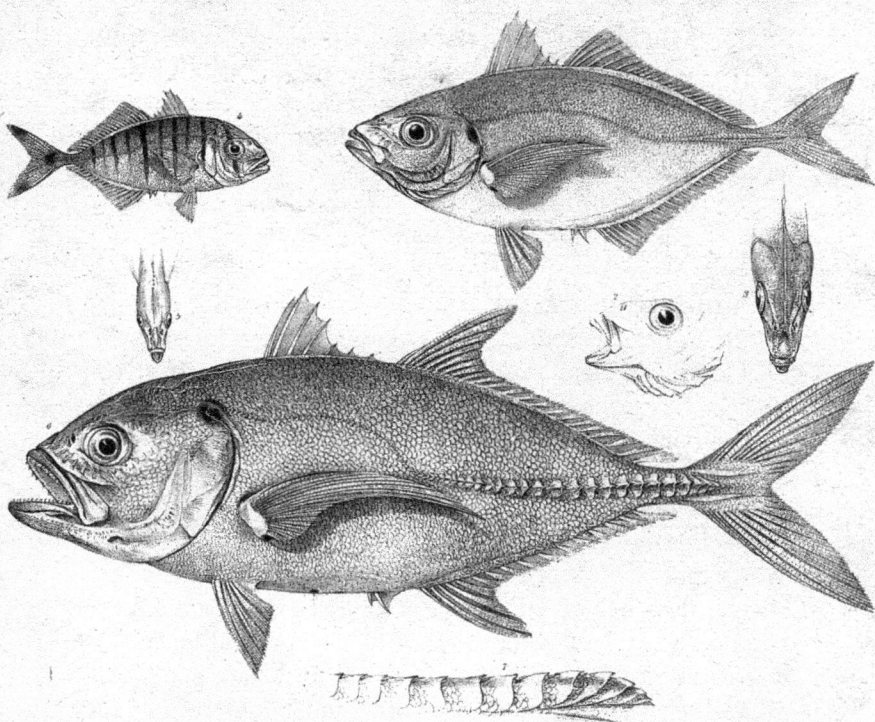

SMOKED PALLINUP MULLET

In 1841, the artist Robert Neill wrote that the flat-nosed mullet was the finest fish in New Holland and I completely agree. Mullet is seriously underestimated in this modern society that seems to want to consume only bland, white-fleshed fish.

Salt was shaking his head as each glossy specimen surfaced with the net.

'Mullet!' I shouted with glee. 'We're not sending these to Perth, Salt! I can sell all of them down at the Sunday market.'

'On your head be it,' he muttered.

'I can sell anything I'm enthused about. Just you wait and see.'

Here are some instructions on how to make hot smoked Pallinup mullet. Soak the fillets, skin on, in a strong brine for twenty minutes. Drain and coat lightly with olive oil. If you want, you can season the fillets with lemon pepper.

If you have a fish smoker then things are already looking good. If not, you will need a wok with a lid and a wire rack. Put some wood shavings or plain tea leaves in the bottom of the wok or smoker, place the mullet on the rack above the shavings, put the lid on and smoke that Pallinup mullet!

Remember not to place the fish smoker's little metho burner on your best friend's plastic outdoor table. It will quietly melt straight through the table and then set fire to her handbag that is underneath the table, destroying the handbag and all of its contents and testing an otherwise good friendship. If this is your modus operandi then it is cheaper to go out for dinner.

Smoked mullet should be piled high on a plate and eaten with your fingers, shared with friends at the end of a sunny Sunday. Peel the smoky, oily flesh away from the skin and put it in your mouth.

DEVOURING THE DODO

A few years ago, camping by the sea in the back of a refurbished refrigerator truck with a solar-generated DVD player, I saw *The End of the Line*. It was with some apprehension that I watched this documentary about the potential collapse of the world's fish stocks. I thought the marine conservationists would be gunning for fisherfolk like me, considering I was working the inlets full-time.

By the end, I realised that the movie actually supported what I'd been thinking about for a while. Selling fish at the markets was already a weekly exercise in informing customers where their food came from, how readily available it was and whether or not it was a sustainable resource. So I rang a marine conservation society and asked them for their sustainable seafood shopping guide. The guide is the size of your average driver's licence and, once I explained what I did for a living, they sent me a wad of about a thousand copies.

The guide is not too bad for accuracy, with only a couple of local glitches. When I showed it to Grievous, he said that although pilchards were listed on the guide as a sustainable fish, pilchard stocks are still recovering from a disease that swept through the Southern Ocean twenty years ago and he questioned their inclusion in the guide. Looking at their traffic light system (red – don't buy it, yellow – aw, maybe, green – sustainable), another commercial fisher said, 'Yeah, well it's okay but there's some species in here that I wouldn't bother working because there aren't enough around to make any money out of.' This is fisherfolk lingo for 'scarce' and therein is the key to the health of the small-scale, family-dominated fishing industries. Economics and long-term sustainability are intrinsically linked. If fish stocks decline for any reason, commercial fishers will go elsewhere until they have recovered.

This kind of self-regulation doesn't happen throughout the fishing industry though. Recently a restaurateur in Japan paid $1.7m AUD for a single bluefin tuna. Yes. One point seven million bucks; about the same you'd pay for an eighth of an acre in Port Hedland. This price and the media prestige that came with it troubled me and that is before I start to rant about the cost of real estate in Western Australia.

Salt and I went out fishing for crabs recently because he'd heard from old Kailis that blue mannas were fetching an obscene amount per kilo in Perth; twice what we normally sold them for. He got so excited about the price offered that he completely forgot about the breeding season. Every pot we pulled up was full of berried female crabs and we had to chuck them all back. We didn't make a single dollar. That was why the price was so high of course. Supply and demand. The market works the same way with gold, except you don't have to kill gold.

Aside from the prestige and publicity associated with the highest price ever paid for a single fish, the restaurateur acknowledged that at $7,600 a kilogram, he wouldn't be turning a profit. But the prestige factor only served to reinforce that bluefin tuna's worth will rise as its population in the world's oceans becomes scarce. According to the researchers of *The End of the Line*, there is already stockpiling going on to anticipate this event. Consider what a legal market in rhinoceros horn, elephant tusk or tiger penis would look like; then consider that doomed bluefin. Despite all that we know about the extinctions of the previous two centuries, rare creatures are still worth more dead than alive.

ANOTHER FISH AND BICYCLE YARN

The day before a trip to Katanning on family business, Salt helped me lug two huge iceboxes onto the back of my ute. So the King George whiting, snook and herring came for a drive too.

'Why don't you try and sell some fish up there?' he asked.
'Whenever I go inland with fresh fish, I stop at the pub.'
'Will they buy fish?'
'Dunno, never asked.'

I drove through shocking yellow fields of flowering rape, pondering, as you do on a long drive alone. Someone told me recently that the rape flower is the closest colour to pure yellow in the light spectrum. It's pretty hard not to feel emotionally moved, stunned even, by that vision of gold, punctuated by moments of emerald trees. In reality, it's a hard-nosed agriculture with a multinational at the helm. And how do you market *rape oil* to the modern-day gatherers, the mothers, wives and other females of the species? Better still, how do you market *genetically-modified rape oil*? There must be a way ... ah yes, in one stroke of marketing genius, it gets renamed something pretty, rounded, innocuous – *canola*.

I stopped at a wheatbelt hotel looming on the corner of a dying street, a grand old shady lady clad in turquoise peeling paint. Yellow tape roped off the groaning veranda – 'Do not cross. Party scene.'

I went into the front bar. It was ten in the morning and

the balloons were already up. Sky Channel blared. The bar was packed. I forgot it was Grand Final day.

'I was wondering,' I asked the barmaid, 'if the cook wants to buy some fresh King George whiting fillets?'

The bar went silent beneath the racket of the TV and everyone turned to stare at me. I felt like backing up with my hands in front of my face – or perhaps going on the offensive – 'I'm licensed to fish and insured to sell!' whilst waving around a pike.

She explained to me, waving her jingling silver jewellery and spider tattoos in the direction of the coast, that the frozen fish van comes once a week to deliver them basa. So thanks but no thanks.

I drove on to the next town, to another pub. A man on the footpath was doing something strange with one of those blower things. He was blowing dust out of its bag and into an ice-cream container. Dust was going everywhere, all over the walls. It made no sense to me. I got out of the car and asked him about the fish anyway.

He looked at me as though I were the strange one (a curly-headed hippy from the coast trying to flog some fish, perhaps). It didn't go well. 'Nah, I fink we're right love,' he folded the words around his beard and occasional teeth. 'We get basa from the fish bloke once a week.'

Basa sometimes gets the cruel moniker of Mekong blind mullet. As a freshwater catfish imported from one of the most polluted rivers in the world, it doesn't have a terrific reputation. But it is bland tasting and very cheap.

After that I gave up trying to sell fresh fish to sea-starved inlanders and focussed on my original reasons for the visit. On my way out of Katanning a few hours later, I stopped in at a great little antique shop on the highway. The proprietor stood out in the sun, polishing something brass, listening to the footy on a transistor radio.

Whilst chatting, my attention was drawn to the bicycle. Ooh, a bicycle! And what a darling. A proper postman's bicycle from the 1960s. Bright red and white! Back brakes! I couldn't believe my find. It turned out she just loved King George whiting. She did me a great deal for a kilo of fillets.

THE SALMON ARE HERE

'There's been rumours,' Salt said as he drove away from the fishing camp. 'It happens every year. *Oh, there's salmon over at Cheynes. There's salmon at Nanarup. They're coming.* Every bastard's heard a story about the salmon coming.'

The massive schools of salmon that work their way from east to west against the Leeuwin Current are on the minds of every southern fishing community this time of year. Despite the death of the local cannery businesses – now the salmon is usually sold as pet food or cray bait – the salmon arrival still bugles the age-old call – the seasonal harvest, the abundance.

I visited Cable Beach, where the Southern Ocean rolls in and deposits improbable boulders onto limestone plinths. A family of enthusiastic Noongars followed me down the steps, bristling with fishing rods. We reached the sea together. We all saw the small school of gathering salmon in the window of a wave and cried out, 'There they are!'

People make some fatal mistakes on the rocks during salmon season. The fish can mass at the base of granite slopes made slick with black algae. The southern sea is dangerous and unpredictable. Swell smashes into the rocks and occasionally, that bigger rogue wave will wash a hungry fisher away.

After the yellow flowering of the Christmas tree comes the red flowering gum. These scarlet blooms herald the salmon run. The Menang people used to get together this time of year with neighbouring peoples to discuss things. From the ranges of the east and the inlets and tingle forests of the west, they came to talk business: the hatched, matched and dispatched, who was annoying who, and what the season was producing – and there was always enough food for everyone because the salmon were here.

During World War II, Dan Hunt, an ex-copper, realised that the soldiers were tiring of bully beef and saw an excellent opportunity to sell salmon. This was the real beginning of the south coast commercial salmon industry. Fishers began to seine net salmon from the beaches. They used the detritus of war including blitz trucks for driving on the beaches and camouflage nets for catching the fish. Someone used an armoured tank to cart nets and fish over the sandhills. Dan Hunt flew a spotter plane, looking for big schools of salmon and, when he spotted a mob near a licensed beach, he would write its location on paper, wrap it around a stone and throw it down to the camp.

The original purpose of the salmon camp was to catch salmon in huge seine nets. When a school comes into the bay, the fisher men and women row a boat around the school, spooling out the salmon net. Then they use tractors, four-wheel drives and bare hands to drag the net onto the beach. Big trucks from the processing factories drive onto the white, kelpy sands of the beach and are loaded up with salmon.

The salmon season was a financial bonanza for the fishing families, who often struggled for the remaining year. Because of the money, squabbles were inevitable as fishers scrambled for position on the most lucrative beaches. Sometimes they waited weeks for a big school to come along the coast. Salt's mate remembers the windscreen getting shot out of a truck by an irate competitor who had someone shoot a net *inside* of his own seine.

Eventually it was organised so that certain licence holders stayed on their own beach and no other commercial salmon fisher could work that beach. And that's the way it is today ... only those camps tend to be a lot quieter than they were in the heyday of the south coast salmon fishery.

ARRIPIS TRUTTA

During a period of time working another job with a more predictable income, I wasn't always available as Salt's deckie. He retired to the salmon camp and rang every other day entreating me with stories of massive schools of fish.

'There's salmon all around the bay. And mulies and birds working them. And there is mullet too, in the pool, right in front of me. The weather's great. D'yer wanna go fishin'?'

He knew that I was moving house this day but just thought he'd let me know, in case I was getting tired of lugging freezers and wardrobes on to the trailer.

'I can't come out today.' I looked at the sky. Mares' tails and mackerel scales. 'I can come out tomorrow but it looks like it will blow up by then.'

'Nah, it'll be fine tomorrow. Bloody gorgeous out here right now. Can't do a shot for mullet anyway. Too much weed onshore at the moment.' So why did Salt ring me with mullet stories if we couldn't even catch them?

Because he knew my penchant for mullet and that I was moving house.

It transpired that this was the first and only occasion I've out-forecast Salt. The next morning was wet and howled with a dirty south-easterly that turned around to the south-west by lunchtime to make a mess of the foreshore in town. The whole harbour was a creamy slush and seagulls fought the wind, like scraps of paper, on their daily flight from the rubbish tip to the new entertainment centre.

'Never known you to be so wrong about the weather and me so right,' I crowed to Salt. 'No thanks. Maybe on the weekend.' See? When not officially working for Salt, I can go fishing when I feel like it and I can give some lip. A few months before, this kind of behaviour would have earned an entirely different outcome.

'Weather shithouse out here,' he sent a message back, and then slapped me down anyway. 'Don't get too smug about 4casting. Once in 5 years no Einstein stuff.'

I think Salt turned seventy-five this year and he knows his weather. The only other time I've heard a dodgy forecast from him is when he's trying to keep me out at sea in order to get the nets picked up a bit later than I would like. 'Oh the wind will drop at sunset,' he says when he's trying to bluff me into staying in a bay where the wind is blowing us into the surf.

Salt stayed out at the camp and watched the salmon swim in and out of the bay. The market has crashed for this cheap, coarse fish. People are importing Asian fish or just not liking the flavour of Australian salmon. So Salt's camp has morphed into a kind of seasonal village for retired salmon fishers.

When the weather calmed down, I drove to the camp. We launched the dinghy into the surf and motored off to hook some salmon and set the whiting net at Dunsky's. On the way is Forsyth Bluff where the southern swell crashes into barnacled granite. The heads, where granite protrudes from the land to create the separate bays, are always a good spot to troll for salmon. We watched for birds working. They are usually after the pilchards or whitebait, pushed to the surface by bigger schools of predatory fish. Salt ran the boat through the middle of one of these mobs, against the chop bouncing off the Bluff.

Arripis trutta ... catching salmon is visceral and exciting: that sure yank against nylon, the fight that turns my fingers raw, the blue heads of the salmon surfing through the wake wave behind the boat, shrieking birds and finally hauling a big fish onto the deck. It's enough to make me want to down a Bloody Mary at the end of the day and call myself Hemingway.

On we went, the boat swilling with brine and the blood of salmon, past The Eyes, a ghostly pair of deep, round holes worn into the cliff's face, past the murder scene where the burnt-out four-wheel drive crouched on the rocks, on past the turquoise waters of Shelley Beach and into Dunsky's Bay.

We set the whiting nets and waited, watched the smoke from a fire at West Cape Howe move over the sky. 'We should sell those salmon all right down the markets,' said Salt. 'Ten bucks each.'

On our way back to the camp we came across some albatrosses who were working the whitebait and pilchards with muttonbirds. The big ocean birds waddled over the water as we neared them, took off into the sky and settled again. Muttonbirds buzzed the boat, shearing so close that one nearly touched my hair.

'I'll do the next season at Pallinup,' said Salt. 'Then I might just finish up.' He looked at the box of beautiful King George whiting. 'Though pulling up those big bastards makes me think I'll hang up my boots when I hang down my head. Days like this, I wouldn't call the king my uncle.'

MIRRONG, MUGIL, MULLET

We used Salt's salmon camp for a while as our base to go out hunting King George whiting. This day though, was all about sea mullet.

When mullet spend a season in the estuary they get pretty fat but when they get outside in open waters they get leaner because they are chased around by sharks and dolphins. Despite this exertion, their oil content remains obscene. In an anthropologist's terms, the calorific exchange in the process of catching and eating sea mullet is exceptional.

In the camp, the grassed area by the sea was packed with caravans, ancient buses and tents. Parsley told Salt about the sea mullet he'd been watching.

'Oh yeah, I seen them. A huge school and really moving, they were. I was out on the quad bike at six yesterday morning and followed them around the bay. Then they stopped at the pool right here. They were all jumpin' outta the water ...'

'Why didn't you ring me?' Salt looked like he was in great pain. His face was a bit red. Parsley was the third person who'd told him about this school of sea mullet.

'Well, we got the net onto the boat –'

'With the cork line and lead line back to front –'

'And then they were gone! Dunno where they went. Out to sea, I s'pect.'

'Then they came back this mornin'. Why didn't you ring

me this mornin'?' Salt leaned against the trailer and kicked the wheel. Hard.

'They'da been gone by the time you got here.'

'I can be here in twenny,' said Salt. He was beyond looking pained. He wanted to hurt someone, I could tell.

'Your van's here, Salt. Why don't you stay here and keep an eye out for them yourself?'

I like Parsley and I was beginning to feel sorry for him.

I've known Parsley for a long time and only ever on the stretch of beach between Muttonbird and Migo islands. His face is brown and cracked and permanently crowned with an old beanie. Even though he owns a house in town, Parsley seems happiest in his ancient caravan by the beach or camping on a friend's farm. During the off-season he works fencing. He is kind and gossipy and rather old-fashioned. Salt asked him recently if he wanted some fresh plums from his overloaded tree and Parsley replied, 'Oh, no thanks, Salt. I've got no taste for those new things. I like the old things, the tinned plums.'

After the excitement of the salmon season beginning, things quietened down at the camp.

'I don't even want to come out here sometimes,' Salt said, as he did the country fisherman's version of an intergalactic space drive: dodging peppermint trees in the dark on a sandy black track, boat and trailer *kerthunking* behind us. 'We used to all sit up in the shed, all get together at night, cook and drink piss and carry on ... now everyone is in their own caravan at eight o'clock, watching TV.'

They haven't been fishing either. It seems at the moment that there is no market for this oily, fishy fish. After the salmon season, most south coast camps work the herring schools but, due to the recent decline in the cray industry, the local processors are not buying bait fish and will only buy herring for human consumption if it is iced down by the beach seiners. At dawn.

One family out of the three who usually work this beach hasn't turned up this year. Salt Sister had a baby a few weeks before, so she won't be swimming out the anchor for the herring net and there's not even enough reason to hire a tractor.

Salt may have been annoyed at missing out on such a beautiful school of sea mullet but he is probably even more annoyed at seeing such an abundance of salmon swim by the camp that there is no point in catching. Who in the whole world could possibly want tons of cheap, sustainable run fish, drenched in omega-3s from the clean Southern Ocean? Anyone?

AND THEN THERE WAS AN OCTOPUS

An octopus in the net out near Migo Island is a good starting point for our weekly argument.

'He'll do for bait.' That's Salt. 'We're going out hookin' tomorra.'

My son, Stormboy, who knows these things, says, 'Octopus are so smart, if they weren't underwater, they would have learned how to make fire.'

Tom Robbins hypothesised that because octopus are so emotional that they can become apoplectic when overwrought, it is perfectly plausible that an octopus might die of embarrassment.

'Bite 'im between the eyes and turn 'im inside out,' says Salt.

I remember Dunedin and the lovely wahine Donna Toa. She told me stories of living on octopus and fish from the bay and described to me the traps they set.

My take this night in the channel near the island?

'I'll eat him. Lightly blanched, dropped in vinegar. Otherwise the octopus goes back. Bait? No way.'

I put the octopus in the box with a lonely squid and shut tight the lid. Half an hour later in the midst of hauling the night nets in and the motor cutting on the windward side of a snarly reef:

'Jesus Fucking Christ!'

The critter was crawling over my bare feet and heading for the sides. I watched that octopus. The dog watched too. How the hell did it get out of the box? The lid was still on.

Stormboy, the dog and I watched it creep along, tentacle after tentacle. We didn't say anything to Salt.

We headed to shore, stowed the nets and crunched onto the beach. Salt was trying to lift the new two-stroke's propeller out of the sand. I watched the octopus heave his way up the side of the boat. He got one tentacle over the side.

Salt was going over the side too. He saw the octopus plop into the water under the fluorescent light, fly past his feet, heading for the open sea.

'Didya see that occy? Bastard got away.'

'Yep.'

'You were watching the whole time.'

'Yep.'

STINGRAY STEAK

Standing waist-high in the turquoise waters of Whalers Cove I saw the stingrays come a'hunting, their shadowy pirate sails varnished and black. It was a nervous moment but they swept around me in wide arcs, looking for herring and whitebait along the seashore.

I've loved stingrays since that encounter. I feed them mullet frames from the beach and try to keep the dog from retrieving them. We've pulled up a few in the nets too. Most of the time I let them go, much to Salt's annoyance. When they have munched on every other fish in the net, I take them home and eat them.

At the Sunday markets I have an English customer who relishes stingray. She poaches it and serves it up with butter and capers. I use my own antipodean's recipe.

Hopefully you've got a Salt or a fisherwoman in the neighbourhood who can deal with the killing and cutting of a stingray because landing it involves lots of blood and wriggling and squabbles, especially in a little boat.

The flesh is a strange, grainy texture with a sheet of cartilage through the wing holding the whole thing together. Cut the wings straight down, into one-inch steaks. A sharp, flexible knife will deal with the skin and the cartilage. Make up a mix of soy sauce, olive oil and freshly grated ginger. Marinate the stingray steaks in this mix for a few hours. Then cook the stingray steaks quick and hot on a barbeque.

HOW TO FEED A FISHERMAN

Apart from sea mullet and salmon cooked in huge slabs in a frypan, Salt's idea of culinary delight is mustard pickles or corn relish on white bread with cold meat, or boiled potatoes and lamb chops. He also likes Spam.

I told Salt I may be late getting to the fishing camp. Just not how late. Originally I was intent on getting to Pallinup in time to set nets but I got stuck up the mountain I'd been climbing. As soon I was within range, I sent him a message to say that I'd be there before dawn.

Salt and I have had plenty of conversations about me being late.

Sandy was standing by the fire a week later and laughing about the debacle. 'Oh yeah, Salt, I had one of those deckies who could never turn up on time come Saturday morning.'

Salt looked at me. 'We've always had a problem with Saturday mornings, haven't we Sarah?'

Sandy said, 'I'd ask him on Fridays, *You going to the pub tonight? Nah, nah*, he'd say. The next day I'd be waiting at the jetty for him. By seven thirty I'd have to drive around to his house and wake him up.'

'Seven?' I said. 'Seven is a completely respectable hour. Who can't make it to a boat ramp by seven? Now, four thirty on a Saturday morning is a different matter.'

Salt groaned and rolled his eyes at me.

'Well. Four thirty. C'mon Salt. It's not always achievable. It means three forty-five out of bed after sitting with my friends around a fire, playing guitars till one in the morning.'

'Yeah, I always hate the summer crab season around you social butterflies,' he said.

On this occasion, I didn't make it by dawn. After sleeping under a rock in the dirt, it took me till lunchtime the next day to trek across the north face of the mountain to the car park. Hungry, scratched and bruised, with an eye suffering from a misanthropic spider, I got a message from Salt once I'd arrived back at my car: 'Eight boxes.'

Damn. The last time he caught that much I was camping on Breaksea Island. He's never caught that many fish when I'm around. At this point I began to entertain the women-and-bananas-on-boats superstition.

I met him at the roadhouse on his way into town. He was sleeping in his car when I pulled over. I showed him some bruises as evidence of my mountain misadventure but he was having none of it.

'You know, last night the caravan went up on three wheels in that storm. This morning I was trying to pick up, and nearly rolled the boat in the wind. I had to tie the net onto the bow and pick up fish and all. And that was only the first fuckin' net! The boat filled with water. I had to come in. Sandy saw me come in and asked if I needed a hand pickin' up the other two nets. Of course I said no but he insisted.'

Sandy had then helped Salt unmesh his fish and pack them into boxes. Once Unruly had finished with his own catch, he came and helped too.

'You owe them both a slab,' Salt told me. 'They were bloody good blokes, those two. I always thought fishermen are bastards but those two ... they're really good, they are.'

I dropped off a carton of beer to Unruly's shack last week. It was a surreptitious operation; it had to be at an hour when I knew the two fishermen wouldn't be there to refuse my gift of thanks. I drove past the shack lands, through deep puddles in the chewed-out track and into the mallet country.

I pulled into the clearing where their shack stood among the mallets and burnt out car wrecks. They had a fireplace crafted from a truck's brake drums and inside the three-sided shed was a tent, a cooker, some wire beds. I've seen them cooking up in the evenings. Unruly will boil potatoes and fry sausages, or Sandy will make a kind of cabbage, carrots and steak meal. I placed the carton on the bush kitchen bench and left.

Unruly and Sandy had a late start out on the inlet the next day. Later as they were chopping ice and packing fish into boxes on the shore, I wandered down to say thank you, for saving Salt in his moment of need (and probably his life) but they both looked at me like I was quite superfluous, nodded and went back to their work. They didn't see their heroism as anything other than ordinary behaviour and I wonder if they found my gratitude necessary.

It's a code that I'm still unsure how to navigate. 'Fishermen don't ask for help,' Salt has told me more than once. 'And if anyone offers, refuse them. But always step up when yer needed.'

How do you work that one out? And how do I renegotiate it, being a fisher*woman*?

Anyway, the irony of my absence while Salt got into trouble on the inlet was that instead of getting sacked for a no show, I'd proved myself indispensable. There was a price apart from the beer though.

'Those blokes, they are the best fishermen I've worked with for twenny years. I want you to put a feed on for them at the end of the season, Sarah. We'll invite them over to my camp for the night. Give them a real slap-up feed. Whaddaya reckon?'

Salt was quite definite about the 'nibblies' he wanted me to provide. 'Some cubes of cheese and bits of pineapple on toothpicks. I know you don't like Spam but they do.' He hassled me about it all week, even ringing me while I was shopping. 'So get them some Spam, okay? And those little green cocktail onions. Yeah, and maybe some bickies too.'

OF HARBOUR AND INLET

In the inlets, fishers set their nets at dusk. They return before dawn the next morning to pick them up. Inlets are a world unto themselves known by those who brave the tigersnakey reeds to be contrary places, full of dark secrets and seeping beauty. For a lot of the year, we fish 'outside' in open waters like the Sound. Then the rains begin. Rivers flush out their booty — black bream, tarwhine, mulloway, herring, whiting and mullet into the swelling inlets. The sandbars open to admit the ocean fish like sea mullet, skippy and salmon trout. Gathering tannins from the melaleucas make the water nice and black.

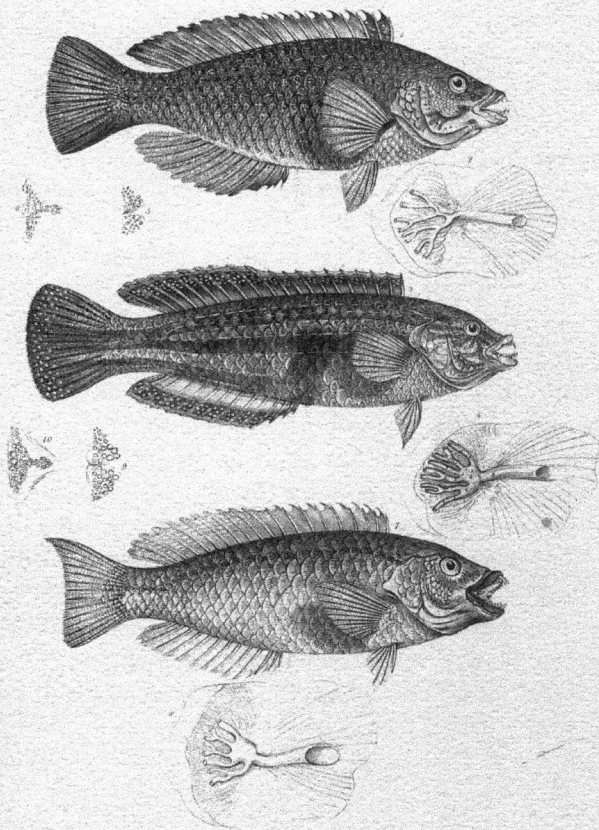

GONDWANA MER

We live on an island continent and yet, for Australians, it's always been about the land. There are different ways of thinking about these two spaces, water and land.

I asked Salt once where the Menang fish traps were because I knew they were around Oyster Harbour somewhere and had never visited them.

'Somewhere over there,' he gestured vaguely towards the shore between the two river mouths.

We were setting four-inch nets to catch the big black bream and sea mullet that swim down the rivers with the rains. Near the river mouths, the briny lies over the top of stained and cold river water. Sometimes, when the tide is rising, the two waters flow in different directions. Big rains also mean unexpected treasure and detritus in the mesh: the skulls of ancient creatures, riverside prunings and pieces of the old jetty encrusted with barnacles.

Salt watched the movements of the other commercial boats. 'What's their number?' He reckons when he gets his cataracts fixed he won't need me any more.

'Dunno, Salt. Why don't we just go over and say gidday?'

He shook his head quickly. Fishermen, they're a weird mob (and that is my nod to you, Nino). The Fisheries Department have it all over the commercials because the fishermen don't always communicate terribly well with each other, in case they give their secret flathead or mullet spot away.

'Watch out for the rocks around these shallows,' said Salt.

I was on the tiller while Salt played out the nets and I winced every time I felt the prop thud against a stone.

A week later, a friend showed me where the old Menang fish traps are. The tides were very low, so it was a good time for exploring the sand flats. Giant marri trees grew right at the water's edge. The reed beds were strewn with beach plastic, bleached and polished flotsam of upriver banksias and pine. Samphire crowded in crimson and green along the lower ebbs.

The stones of the fish traps are a conglomerate that looks like it is still being formed: rich ochre, nearly black in colour. The traps were scattered, breached, so as not to waste fish. The outlines of the convex arcs are still visible in the long shallows of the bay. My friend and I scrambled around and found old and recent camping spots and fresh, wild oysters, plump and intense with iodine and liquor. I looked out to the arcs of stone and remembered Salt's words from the week before.

'Watch out for the rocks around here in the shallows.'

That day we could see the traps in their beautiful, timeless formation because the tide was so low. The only time that Salt has ever set nets in that area is when the tide is high enough to get the boat in and out. He has never seen the traps or known where they were because whenever he's been in the vicinity, they have been covered with silty water.

A historian said to me recently, 'I can't believe such and such explorers both missed the mouth of the Murray. Couldn't even see a river mouth. They must have been asleep.'

'It's actually really easy to miss a river, at sea,' I told him. 'The river mouths just sort of fold into the shore. You often won't see one until you are looking right down it.'

The historian is essentially a land man. He's been a farmer for fifty years and has spent a lifetime negotiating the sea from the land. Salt has spent a lifetime negotiating the land from the sea. It takes a bit of a shift in perspective.

I find it strange that, for a continent totally surrounded by sea, we spend so much time ignoring it. Once the dependence on sea highways lessened and the roads and rail prevailed, placenames began to lose that salty flavour: King George Sound became Albany, the Swan River Colony became Perth. We stand at the water's edge and dream but beyond the lacy breakers is the domain of itinerants, roamers, pirates and guys like Salt. Interesting though, that after seven thousand years or so of the fish traps being built in Oyster Harbour, the fishermen still set nets in the same location. Whether they approach the sea from the land, or the land from the sea, the Menang people and the estuarine fishers know where the black bream are.

PALLINUP

I drove the old ute through the night to Pallinup. I'd just had a new windscreen fitted so the vision was good until the fuses started blowing. After that it was the moon, some white line hallucinations and the chilly radiations from Venus that got me there. I coasted down into a geological anomaly of rainbow-layered spongolite stone, a basin hollowed out by watery millennia, to the soundtrack of drumming rain and my car's rattly tie rod ends. When I got to the fishing camp perched on the paperbark edges of the inlet I saw that Salt had lit a fire in anticipation. A perfect welcome for a frayed spirit is a fire spitting with raindrops, and a decent cup of tea.

'You've obviously been eating a lot of carrots,' was all he said in reference to my dark arrival. He had already set the nets for mullet and bream. It was my job to help him pick up before dawn and drive the catch back into town. The lightning storms and glass-off of the previous week were replaced by howling easterlies, constant drizzle and other rhetoric. It's the kind of misty rain that lets me think I'm waterproof until the moment of realisation that I'm soaked through. A bit like drinking really. I went to my tent quite sodden.

It was still dark when my alarm clock went off with ditzy, electronic muzak. I crawled out of the tent to meet the dawn The tinny was talking, a metallic splash against her sides with every little breath of water. Salt had made some tea.

The Pallinup Estuary had the highest level of nutrients out of the south coast estuaries sampled in 1988 – attributed to the mandate to clear one million acres a year and then smother it with good ol' superphosphate. The estuary also has one of the highest salt levels. This water is so briny that few fish other than mullet or bream can survive it when the sandbar locks them away from the sea. Sometimes the bream develop salt burns on their bodies. Yet this extreme salt content also produces the cleanest flavoured and most splendid-looking sea mullet.

We pulled up a lot of mullet that morning. Salt reckoned it was the wind aerating the water that was bringing the fish in. I just thought we were a little bit blessed.

'Mullet!' is my refrain when the fat, gleaming fish splash to the surface. I began to sound like the Energizer Bunny's lacklustre companion an hour later when we were still pulling in mullet. The fish hit the nets hard and then roll in them, so they can be a job to get out.

'What's wrong? Your battery run out?' Salt asks. '*Oh, mullet!*' He mimics me. '*Look! Another mullet! Yay, oh joy!* I just want to know where the fucking bream are. They're fetching eight bucks a kilo at the moment.'

The water was muddy from the constant turbulence. Pale stretch marks laced her reaches. Water slopped over the stern as Salt reversed the boat against the wind. I hate that, it makes me unsteady on my pins. The wind strengthened and the pelicans began 'scaling' the mullet with their beaks, trying to rip them out of the nets. In the end we hauled the whole lot up and took the boat into shore to unmesh the rest. The water churned golden olive, boiling away from the outboard motor.

Salt told me poaching stories while we wrestled the mullet from monofilament and iced them down in the red plastic bins. 'Pullet, Sandy and Nails were down the pub in Denmark skiting about how they were gonna shoot the mouth of the Wilson's for snapper. They were at the pub all night carrying on, told everyone what they were gonna do, the idiots. Just before dawn they got down to the mouth, it'd been opened that day, see. Pullet said later that no bastard woulda recognised him if they saw him cos he was wearin' a balaclava! Pullet's the biggest fucking bloke I've ever seen, you'd know him the moment you laid eyes on him. But at least he had a balaclava on.'

Salt told me stories of his father, poacher of legend. The Fisheries officer in those days rode a bicycle with the aim of arriving silently to witness Salt Senior's nocturnal fishing crimes. One night, he rode that bike twenty kilometres to Torbay Inlet, where it was illegal to fish, to catch him out. Salt Senior was ready for him. The wily, one-armed fisherman watched from shore as the inspector waded out through the silty mud of the inlet and pulled up a whole cork line. No leads, no net, just a rope with corks attached.

In the archives of the State Library, the enmity between these two men forever lies detailed in the annual Fisheries reports archives. 'Salt Senior came in to pay his fishing licence today and threw five shillings on the counter. He said nothing and nor did I.'

I feel very lucky to be witnessing the work of these briny dynasties firsthand. After unmeshing the fish and downing a breakfast of hot coffee and an apple, I drove the one hundred and fifty kilometres back to town and lugged the bins full of iced-down mullet onto the truck for Perth.

'It's great at the depot,' I told my dad. 'You get to see all the other fishermen's bins and check out who is catching what and how much.'

Dad laughed. 'You are beginning to sound like the rest of that bloody mob.'

Jordie's one of the two other fishers who have been working the Pallinup since May. He's a tall, raw-boned man with a vulpine smile. 'I'm nearly sick of the inlet, mate,' he told Salt. He doesn't normally say much. He blurted this out, a moment of odd candour for the quiet fisherman.

'Yeah, it gets like that towards the end of the season,' said Salt.

'Do you get bored?' I asked Jordie.

'Yep, after fixing nets or whatever, milling around all day, I'll go for jaunts into the bush. But I never see anything worth shooting,' he laughed.

'Have you been up through the valley?' I asked. 'Where the scarp is all hollowed out?'

It's ancient, high country swallowing down to the estuary. The sandbar at the east end stops the wild ocean from rushing in. You can understand how the land has changed just by looking at it. It's the water, running down between the hills and loosening massive tracts of dirt into the sea. The place reminds me of Madura Pass, near the Nullarbor Plain, where you can see the edges of the world, the curve of the earth and the glacial pace of the friction between land and water. Eleven thousand years ago, the loss of country to the sea as she swelled and flooded the land marked the rise of weapon technology, changed clan boundaries from one season to the next and is remembered in the flood narratives of the Noongar. Maybe in the future, when it happens again, it will be a real estate issue. The mad, ultramarine blue of leschenaultia flowers against red spongolite, is a contrast to all this millennial longevity.

'I've tried but the midgies drove me back,' said Jordie.

'Not enough bats around to eat all the midgies,' said Salt.

'There's been heaps of bats here in years past,' agreed Jordie. 'Now, no bats and shitloads of midgies.'

Both fishermen nodded.

These kinds of men have always intrigued me. My fascination is with their innately tough, strangely compassionate natures and their knowledge of natural history. People who fish for a living know more about their prey and their workplace than anyone. They learn by a lifetime of watching. Call it research with vested interest.

Jordie's camp is a tidy array of fish bins, iceboxes, a caravan and a clothesline with only his gloves and a towel slung there. He lives in town normally but, currently undergoing a divorce, he says, 'I really live in the back of my car.'

He fishes the inlet every night except Saturdays, heading out in the early evening to set nets near the mouth of the inlet. On our first day at Pallinup, Salt was throwing his hat and stamping on it. 'He asked me where I wanted to set and I told him! And look! He's fuckin' settin' there – right where I said I wanted to!' Jordie had been setting in the same spot for months. It was just good manners to ask Salt, I think, before he went back to doing what he always did.

Out on the water, we hoisted the prop over his net and went to say hello. Jordie's boat was a little plywood dinghy that he'd built himself, painted warship grey with a stow hatch under the bow and open scuppers at the stern. He stood on deck, resplendent in wet-weather gear, and threw up his arms when Salt asked what he was after.

'Who knows?' His weathered face split into a coyote smile. 'Could be anything. Maybe even some mullet.'

'You ever set up the river, Jordie?' It's illegal for us commercials up there.

'Nah, 'course not, mate. Too many big fat bream up there. Clog the nets. Make a right mess.'

They both chuckled. The conversation meandered. Direct questions receive loaded, abstracted answers. Words, information, spiralled around the weather, the fish, the market price, until both men had the answers they sought and felt they have given little away.

We set Salt's nets against a reddening sky, tying the end of the net to a submerged paperbark and spooling out into the centre of the estuary. Pelicans lurked. Brown ducks with metallic wings busied themselves in the wooded shallows. Evening sun beat against the striped ochre cliffs. A light sou'-wester ruffled the water.

When the keel crunched onto the little beach, I looked

up to Jordie's caravan perched on the edge of the inlet, facing out to the sandbar and beyond it to the ocean. I could smell sausages and frying onions, the scent mingling with the salty broth of the inlet.

GRIEVOUS AND THE BLUNTY BOYS

The year after we were at Pallinup, Grievous and the Blunt brothers got the ballot to fish there. I drove out to the camp on my way east and ended up staying a few days. Samwise smiled quietly when I arrived. The day was freakishly hot and the two brothers sat near a smouldering fireplace. Bullet was reading the newspaper. They'd parked the dusty caravan in the same spot where Jordie's had been and a Jolly Roger fluttered from the mobile phone aerial.

Samwise is always smiling. His hair is wild and long. He has a careless, gappy grin a flattened nose and the feet of a hobbit. His face appears to still be growing; broader, chunkier, jowlier with every smile. His demeanour sidesteps the usual combination of furtiveness and bombast found in the other fishermen I know.

'Doesn't say much, does he?' said Salt, later.

Bullet must have been a stripling when he was a kid. Now he has a Bombers tattoo on his calf, sand-dune thongs on his feet and a buzz cut all over his head. He's been fishing commercially since he was fourteen, like his dad, and his grandad too. He either talks machine-gun style, no room for interjections – or he is quiet, inward – neither state is easy to talk through.

At first I thought Samwise was Bullet's deckie. I didn't realise these two fishermen were brothers, and then Bullet told me they were twins. 'Like chalk and cheese we are,' said Bullet. 'Samwise fishes barehanded and I wear gloves –'

'– nah, I never wear gloves,' said Samwise. 'Except at the beginning of the season when the bream wore my hands out ...'

'He never wears sunnies or a jacket or a hat. Leaves all the knots in the mesh too ...'

'I thought you'd gotten them out for me, Bullet.'

'Bastard to set the next day, nets with twigs and shit in them, knots and shit.'

I went out in the boat one evening with Bullet, setting four-inch mesh for black bream out by the ochre cliffs. Bullet wore khaki waders over his board shorts. He seemed to fold himself over the nets as they rolled out of their nest on the deck and over the shadecloth gunwale, into the olivey wake of the dinghy. He grabbed the tiller to straighten out the boat. The wind kept blowing it off the course he chose. 'Listen how quiet that motor is ... good poaching boat this one. Nice and quiet. If I was the sort that is. So quiet. Four-stroke. Just purrs along. Honda. Bloody great motors. Lead core rope on the net too. No fucking sinkers or lead wraparounds clanking over the side. Net goes out real quiet, real quiet.'

Bullet set three lots of net. The four-inch went across another channel further off where the mullet were and another lot out in the middle of the inlet. Then he motored back to the camp. Samwise was already there, piling mallee roots on the fire.

This season the three commercial fishers took turns to net near the river mouth. It's the most lucrative set in the inlet, catching the fish as they swim into the estuary from the river at night. Samwise had the river mouth that night. The next night was Grievous' turn. Grievous only came out on the nights he had the river mouth.

'He'll be here at ...' Bullet looked at his watch, 'five to five. That's the earliest he's allowed to set. Then he'll drive the one-fifty back to Albany, boat and all. He'll come back about two in the morning to pick up. Fuckin' full-on bloke, Grievous.'

Thought he'd chucked the shits with us the first time he took the boat back to town after setting. But then Samwise said he was going out in the Sound at night to check his leatherie traps.'

'Yeah, that's what he said,' Samwise nodded.

Samwise woke me at four thirty the next morning. Through the window of the tent, he said, 'You up, Sarah?'

He was down at the water's edge, bailing out his tinny by the time I got my act together. I dodged through the paperbarks. Branches dragged at my hair. The moon was gone and Scorpio flexed its tail over the western sky.

'Bullet won't be up for a while yet,' Samwise said.

He gestured for me to climb into the boat while it lay ashore, so my feet didn't get wet. He and Bullet and Salt all do this. Then he pushed off and leapt in, poling with the oar out to deep enough water to let the propeller down.

The river mouth worked all right. Samwise bent over the gunwale as each fat bream appeared, golden like a huge water sovereign, and grabbed them before they fell out of the mesh. He squeezed some fish through the mesh or worked the mono backwards over their gills, holding the fish against his body. Mullet thumped into the bins, thudding their tails against the side in protest. He had one bin for bream and another for mullet. The mullet were huge, nearly as big as Australian salmon. Their gills were often bloodied by the net. Their loose scales fell onto the deck. The eyes of the bream turned downwards.

The little boat, emptied of all its nets overnight, began to fill again. The aluminium insides were stained with mullet oil, algae, seaweed and red gravel dust. 'This ol' girl,' said Samwise. 'I've been using this boat for twenty years now. Never had another boat, could do with another motor though. Always got oars in me boat.' The questionable two-stroke was covered in splatterings of seaweed and slime from the nets. It rocked back and forth as it chugged along. I told him I feel the same way about oars, no matter the motor. When we got to the next net he turned off the motor and used the net to keep the boat in place.

There were a few cobbler and some leatherjackets. And a tailor. Samwise cleaned them on the quiet beach below their camp, surrounded in sculptural red boulders. Pelicans came in for their daily feed, nosing through the paperbarks and waddling up the yellow sand. He threw them the heads and guts. They rolled the cobbler heads around in their beak sacs until they had the spines lying down. Then they swallowed them. I've seen old pelicans with so many holes in their beak sacs from being spiked that they look like colanders.

The twins carried their boxes of fish up the hill to the camp where the ute was parked. The boxes were thirty kilograms, or forty if full of cobbler tails. They each laid out their fish neatly in a six-hundred-litre icebox, counting their catch. Bullet shovelled crushed, salted ice over the top, smoothed it out. He fitted the lid and taped it down with masking tape.

All this time, their conversation was that of brothers working, or people who have spent many years working together. Their sentences were abbreviated, respectful but truncated, agreeably surmised. Quick words, said quietly. A question would answer itself. It was obvious that these words did not involve me but it was a pleasant sound as the twins readied the bins of fish for the Perth trucks, their words like a birdsong, waves breaking, a radio playing somewhere close by.

Samwise got out of his waders, threw them over the washing line and disappeared into the gloom of the caravan. When he came out, he was wearing his good black jeans and a clean t-shirt. He shook my hand shyly. His hands were short and strong, his wrists thickened with old muscle. He got into the ute and left for town. It was about seven thirty in the morning and normally, I would be having my first cup of coffee.

'He'll fish at Wilson's tonight,' Bullet said. 'Hey. You said you wanted to go into Bremer to buy some camera film. I was thinking of doing a drive through there and over to Dillon Bay. Bit of a look around. Wanna come?'

SHACKLANDS

Bullet stopped in at the Bremer Bay servo and bought some bread rolls. We crossed the bar at the river mouth and he drove a fisherman's dodgem through the peppermints. His four-wheel drive sounded like a Sherman tank as it chugged through the gears. On the back tray, the dogs grabbed at branches flying by.

We passed a few other four-wheel drives towing camper trailers. Then the ute slewed through the sandhills until Bullet pulled up on the hard, windswept sand of the next inlet's bar. A flock of plovers rose away from the water in unison as the dogs galumphed about. They settled just as fast, as soon as the dogs swaggered away.

'This is the Gordon,' Bullet said. 'We go fishing here sometimes. Mullet, mostly.' A rough tin shack sat beside the track, 'Whale Villa' spray-painted across the corrugated walls. Inside, the floor was black sand and there was a wire bed with no mattress perched in one corner. Someone had scratched into the windowpane, 'Save a whale, harpoon a fat chick.'

'I'll show you some more shacks, yeah?'

We spent the next five hours driving the beaches, the white sand so fine it squealed beneath the tyres, and cutting across rocky headlands into banksia scrub and black sand. On each remote beach, at the end of another perilous track, there was a shack. Working with a necessity-being-the-mother-of-invention ethos and a rough but perversely finetuned sense of aesthetics, commercial fishers have been building shacks along this coast for generations. They built them with corrugated iron and timber, perched on the edge of beaches, the windows viewing to where the whales loll around and salmon flock into the turquoise bays. Inside every shack there is a kerosene fridge. A rusted half-tonne monster carted out there in the 1940s or '50s, it is likely that the fridges will be there long after the shacks have disintegrated. Some of the fireplace chimneys have been fashioned from corrugated iron and house ancient Metters stoves or potbellies made from welded brake drums. Behind all the fishing shacks are verdant patches and great fig trees vivid against the grey-green hues of the coastal scrub. Ahh. The septic tank.

Some of the fishing shacks were built by farmers or anglers but most are commercial salmon fishing shacks on government leases. These shacks are tangible family trees of south coast fishing families. The list of names tenanting these rusted spider homes makes up that briny heritage. As is every commercial fisher's wont, Bullet was disdainful of the shack dwellers who weren't fisher blue bloods. 'They don't pay any lease fees and then they lock them up so no other bugger can use them. They'll all get knocked down one day when the council chucks the shits and then all the commercials' shacks will get knocked down too.'

We stopped for lunch at Whalebone Beach, just past the stone well that Matthew Flinders' men dug in 1802. Bullet showed me the memorial site of an Aboriginal child and another little cairn created in honour of a fisherman's uncle. A track lined with the skulls and vertebrae of whales led from the beach to a large shed nestled into the sand dunes.

'Follow the yellow brick road.' Bullet led me up a little path made of yellow pavers and coral to a whalebone throne on top of the sand dune. He sat down on the sun-bleached bone and then stood up and shuffled his thongs. 'Sit. Try it out.'

I sat. I could see the roof of the shack and the huge

rainwater tanks, then out to the East and West Barrens, a dark necklace of mountains that looked like they forced their way out of the earth just yesterday. A chalk-white beach, the clearest of turquoise water and the deeper ultramarine blue of the seagrass beds – all this in a perfect curve that went on for miles and miles.

We walked back down the track. Bullet pointed out the succulent gardens and stopped by a profusion of smoky green cotyledons by the rainwater tank. 'They had amazing flowers this year. Bright yellowy orange.'

I realised he must have spent a fair bit of time at this place. 'Oh, yeah. I stay here when I'm squidding for days or weeks if the squid are any good. Old Heberle is fine with me looking after the place. I was here a few weeks ago when those flowers were out. Musta been thirty whales outside my door every day. There was an old bloke here too, staying in the shed. He was a bit weird with me being here at first. He had depression or something. Doctor wouldn't give him any drugs. Told him to come out here for three weeks. Wasn't too happy when I rocked up but he got used to me.'

It was about thirty degrees. The horizon began to haze up with faraway wildfire smoke. The dogs were thirsty. Bullet poured some water into a honey pail for them and Digger bullied the other dog away until he slaked his thirst.

'I like to work in different places. Come out here for a while squidding, then I head out to Wilson's or Pallinup. Get some bream, go sharking out at Doubtful Island. Crabbin' ... Samwise, he just goes to Wilson's every night. He's a bit different to me.'

'Where else do you catch shark?'

'Oh, Muttonbird, Haul Off Rock, Torbay, Groper Bluff, off Waychinicup, Cheynes, Bremer ... everywhere, everywhere.'

He opened the door to the shack. Inside, the concrete floors had been recently swept and someone had left a 'thanks for letting us stay' note and some candles on the wood stove. Bullet nodded. Two kerosene fridges stood side by side. I imagined the split windscreen blitz trucks from the war grinding through the Australian bush, carrying whole families, building materials, nets, tractors, boats and those fridges, out to the salmon camp.

Bullet felt protective over this shack. Someone had forced the lock to the 'master bedroom' and, even though no damage was done, 'It just annoys the crap outta me,' he said. 'People should respect this place.'

Bullet took the makings out of his esky and laid it out on the laminate table. Sliced cheese, a whole cooked chook, tomatoes, the fresh bread rolls, lettuce, butter, salt and pepper. A bottle of chilled lime cordial. The dogs lay on the concrete and panted, tongues lolling.

Six shacks and three swims later, we rolled back into the camp at Pallinup. The dogs were too exhausted by then to rouse each other up. They flopped down under a tree and swept the flies off their bodies with their tails. The hazy horizon that Bullet had commented on earlier turned foggy with smoke. The wind turned suddenly around to the sou'-east. The sky was orange and a fierce, gusting gale whipped up the waters of the inlet.

At five to five it was time to set nets. Grievous and another man drove into the camp with the boat clanking on the trailer behind them, the car stereo blaring out Bryan Adams. Grievous waved out his open window to me. 'Gidday, Sarah!'

He backed down to the water, jumped out of the ute and pushed the boat off the rollers. Then he and Bullet worked out where they were setting while Grievous' quiet mate looked on. The wind blew up even madder and the sky was full of smoke. The river mouth was the hardest set because of the wind direction but it would also be the most productive and there was no way Grievous was going to miss out on that. He'd just had to detour an extra fifty kilometres around the fires at Bluff Creek.

His mate said, 'I think I'll stay on shore.' Everyone laughed. I said, 'I think I will too.'

'Carn Sarah,' said Grievous. 'I've seen you out in worse.'

'I'm a mere tourist today, Grievous.'

Bullet took off for the lee side of the estuary, churning an olive wake behind him. Grievous got into his wet-weather gear. His mate and I watched him head into the river mouth. Water and wind can chuck up some nasty surprises on an inlet but Grievous is beautiful to watch in a boat, lithe and graceful. He shouldered the dinghy into the waves and started throwing the nets into the murky chop, only stopping to steer the boat against the wind.

As I fell asleep that night I heard a flock of swans fly over, singing to each other. I heard Grievous return in the greasy night, about two o'clock, talking to his deckie as they passed my tent. I heard them launch the dinghy and start the motor. The wake chattered against Bullet's aluminium dinghy on the shore.

When I woke again, it was Bullet. 'You up, Sarah?'

The morning was red all over from the smoke hanging in the sky. A molten sun climbed over the sandbar. Bullet hauled in nets in the shelter of the paperbark trees. Their ghostly figures danced against the ochre cliffs and grey green forests. A sea eagle watched us from her paperbark eyrie.

'You've got a pelican in the net,' I said.

'Nah,' said Bullet. 'Never happens.'

He screwed up his sleepy face. 'Hang on. It does. I know who that is.'

It looked like a stump or a stake in the water and there are plenty of those in the inlet. Plenty of pelicans too.

'But this guy is sick. He's got a hole in his neck and he's a bit desperate. If the poor bugger tries to swallow a fish in the net and gets the net too, he won't be able to throw it up again. That's what's happened.'

Bullet pulled fish out of the net and dropped them into the box. We drew closer to the pelican.

'Samwise's got an injured pelican at Wilson's that he looks

after,' Bullet said. 'He calls him Wobbles cos he's got a busted wing. He feeds him every day, makes sure he gets some fish ahead of the others.'

The pelican looked weak and didn't struggle as the boat got closer. It was so still I wondered if it had died. Its beak and wings were wound up in the net, so it looked like an ungainly giraffe trying to drink.

We pulled up alongside. 'You'll have to grab 'im. I'll get the fish out.'

The bird had a large gash on one side of its neck and the wound must have gone right through to its throat because a small black bream clad in nylon fishing net poked through the bloody hole.

I held the bird's wings and beak and felt its heart bleating as Bullet quickly yanked out the fish. I thought he was quite brutal until I realised how much pain and distress I would have caused faffing about, trying to be gentle.

He untangled the fish from the mesh and chucked it in the water. 'Don't wanna keep that one.'

'But it's already cooked!'

He pulled away the nets from the pelican's legs and sat it on the water, gently as if it were a baby. We watched it paddle slowly away.

'Poor bugger needs a bullet,' said Bullet.

The sea eagle hadn't moved, had watched the whole rescue.

MY LIFE IN MAY

Slow windless, misty rain.

Wintergrass. The mice move in and the snakes go underground.

Ocean flattens into frosted glass.

Grevillea flowers unfurl and leaves begin to fall from deciduous trees.

Sunglasses and beanie all day.

School busses return from ferrying the farm kids home, headlights on.

There is a swirling web of change around me, this May. Moving house ... an angler begins a popular campaign to stop us fishing Oyster Harbour ... a friend is dying (fast), crucified with pain ... another diagnoses his own cancer and contemplates the various ways he can suicide and arranges for me to look after his dog, then gets the All Clear and goes fishing instead.

I wake at fiveish on the floor of the fishing shack, to the roar of a dark ocean.

It is cold. I'm about to get wet. It is always a hard moment placing my bare feet on gravel, in the water, on the metal chequer plate deck of the boat.

At Irwin Inlet, the hills blackened and steaming with the burning-off fires, we push the boat over the shallows of weed that remind me of waving sheoak needles. Aboard, we punt with the oars for a hundred metres before I can lower the prop and fire up.

As soon as I get the outboard going, I wouldn't be anywhere else in the world. We motor through the channel, marked out by grey sticks with ice-cream container plastic nailed to them. Sun creeps over the hills and spreads across the water.

Salt deals with the cobbler.

The inlet has a skin of quicksilver.

Mullet.

NAILS' NETS

In the hour before dawn at Irwin's Inlet, the black swans lead their young across the water. There are not enough words to name the shades of silver here. The swan voices drift across the silky inlet. If I were here long enough, I would learn the language of the inlet: the birds mapping the fishing grounds with their calls; the reeds and the tiger snakes and the silt and the mullet all speaking to each other.

Jordie, Nails and Unruly had been setting there for weeks, while Salt and I fished Oyster Harbour, so we were the newbies. This evening they had started early by just a few minutes. There were nets *everywhere*. Salt looked longingly towards the northern end but decided not to risk it.

Jordie motored over to our boat. 'Gidday Salt. Just thought I'd let you know where my gear is.' He made various complicated squiggly gestures with his hands to explain the fine cartography of his nets over the huge body of water. His motor was still running. Salt is so deaf by now that he just looked at Jordie's talking face and nodded regularly to show he understood.

'Where did he say his gear was?' Salt asked me, once Jordie had roared off, headed west and then folded into the forest, up the river to hide his boat overnight.

We set the nets with the easterly blowing the boat across the water and drifted near some tea-tree markers.

'There's a channel coming up.'

'Yeah. Just stay off the bank. That'll be where the Kent River comes out.'

I began to stress about setting the nets across the river mouth but Salt didn't care. 'Some bastard always runs into this net. That's why it's the Irwin's net. Always in fuckin' bits.'

Sure enough, in the morning, the net was broken. Salt was cursing, again. 'How the hell did they manage to run into it *three times*?'

This was about the time I met Nails. I've seen him in the distance but never met him until he came over while we were sorting through the black bream net. He pulled his boat in neatly next to Salt's and put his wader-clad foot on both gunwales to hold them there.

'Hey Salt. Ran into yer net last night. Sorry mate. Woulda fixed it but it was dark. Couldn't see a bloody thing.'

It's a funny kind of honour, the running-into-nets agreement. Even though Salt had nets all around the channel that Nails used to get into the inlet, the onus was still on Nails to rectify the damages. I've seen this before when Salt ran into Bullet's nets in Oyster Harbour. Fishermen are supposed to fix them on the spot, by finding the stray ends of the cork line and tying them back together, but it doesn't always happen.

'Don't worry mate. Shouldna set over there anyway.' Salt was feeling gracious. 'I just couldn't get past everyone else's gear last night.'

Nails' dinghy was a neat little boat with a plywood deck. He stood, one boot on the gunwales and the other amongst his piles of net. He was using rag net, for catching cobbler. A beautifully carved cobbler waddy lay handy. Like most men who have spent their lives on the water, his face was cracked and worn.

'Been gettin' a bit of mullet out in the middle but it's all calmed down now the bar's gone.' Nails meant the sandbar that breaches to let out the inlet flush out to sea, once there is enough rain.

'Did it open by itself?'

'Nah. Council came down and dug it out. We argued for about a week for them to wait until it rose another eight inches. Shoulda gone up over the road really. But the water got just close to the road and they had to breach the bar. Ohhh, the tourists couldn't possibly drive through water!' He flapped his hands and grinned.

The high-water mark was all around the inlet, staining the reeds and paperbark trunks like a bath ring.

Later we happened across a big school of tarwhine. There was one monster, the biggest I've ever seen, his snout all burly and gnarled.

'I almost want to chuck this old man back,' I said to Salt.

'Oh, you're feeling a bit warm are ya?'

'What?'

'Feelin' a bit hot?'

'Huh?'

'*Wanna* go for a swim, do ya?'

That afternoon, Salt asked Jordie where he was setting. They stood in the shallows of the launching beach at Irwin's, water swilling around their boots. Salt was asking because it can get a bit hectic at Irwin's, when four or five other fishers have nets all over the place. The cork lines can get torn up by the propeller and if that happens in the evenings the net flays around in the water and catches nothing.

'I haven't run over anyone's nets for years,' Salt told me for Jordie's benefit.

'Yes, you have.' I can be treacherous like that.

'Oh ... Bullet's. Yeah. Dunno how Nails manages to do it so much. Saw him run over my net next to the marker buoy once. Right in front of me. Ran over it three times last night.'

Jordie nodded.

The next morning, we pushed the boat out of the shallows.

'Water's bright,' said Salt. There had not been much rain to wash the tannin stain down the river.

When we were level with the island, Salt fired up the two-stroke. I stood at the bow keeping an eye out for buoys. Salt knew where Jordie had set, so he throttled it. He wanted to beat the pelicans to his whiting. The chill wind forced into the neck of my jacket. My plastic pants filled out like a clown's. The cold air bit at my eyes, forcing tears.

Then I was face down on the forward deck, surrounded in a clatter of plastic bins, milk crates and the pointy bit of the anchor. The motor was revving and turning the boat in a big lazy arc. Salt lay on the thwart, staring at the sky. The dog had gone overboard.

Still got my teeth? Check.

I climbed down to the stern, eased off the throttle and put it into neutral. The dog swam towards us, shaking water out of his ears. Salt completed an inventory of his body and got to his feet.

'Fuck. Fuck. Fuck.'

'You all right? What happened?'

'Just ran into Jordie's net. Fuck.'

I dragged the dog over the gunwale and he shook the estuary all over me. As we motored over to the nets, a bit slower this time, Salt said, 'The motor was on tilt lock. That's why we stopped so quick. I'm gonna have to find Jordie before he gets to that net and sees what we done.'

We started picking up the whiting net. The dog had forgotten all about his dunking. He looked like he was considering leaping out after the pelicans. Still no sign of Jordie. Finally I saw his white wake, racing from the car park on the west end of the inlet. I watched him go down the channel. 'He's gettin' the other net first.'

Salt seemed quite rattled but not about the nasty fall he'd just had. He can mend bruises and dislodged gall stones but a busted reputation takes a lot longer. Another boat came out of the Kent River. 'Good,' said Salt. 'I can finally blame *something* on an amateur.'

The second net was full of cobbler. Salt used the waddy and I used the pliers.

On our way back, Salt pulled in to where Jordie had nearly finished his cobbler net. 'Jordie, mate. I think I just ran into one of your nets.' Salt's demeanour was one of defeat. He even managed to look sad.

Jordie chucked his buoy onto the deck. 'That's my last buoy in, Salt. I reckon you ran over Nails' net.

'That's 'im is it? That other boat?'

Jordie nodded.

'Well. That's okay then!'

'Yep.'

'Looks like Nails shoulda got out of bed earlier.' They both laughed.

The two fishermen talked for a while, with the boats anchored on the inlet, near the island, cutting the heads off cobbler with filleting knives and throwing them to the beggar pelicans.

MONSTERS AND FIRE FAERIES

We picked up the nets from another inlet at dawn and then I ran with my son Stormboy along the wild deep beach on the other side of the bar. His long hair flipped about over the school uniform he was still wearing from the day before. Lacy teal dumpers crashed into the sandbar. We ran until we came to the beach shack, where we could watch the drifting whales from the veranda.

When the day came a putrid wind blew, and the culprit was the rotting carcass of a leviathan long dead, rolling about in the surf. We thought it was a sperm whale. Further along the beach, another car-sized lump of flesh and bone lay. Further still, its cleansed skull.

Last night we drove with Salt through the banksia scrub and found our way to the quieter side of the sandbar amongst the paperbarks, rolled out some swags in the soft sand. We rowed out into the centre of the inlet and set some net.

I stood on the thwart of the tiny rowboat to punt over crunchy coral shallows. Incessant swell, the startled night call of a wood duck and water rippling against the sides of the boat were the things I heard. I was the tallest point in the whole inlet. Above me the stars blazed and a quarter moon glowed the water into shining steel.

I'm not big on ideas of reincarnation. Perhaps it's because my life can be dramatic enough without invoking Boadicea or an Egyptian priestess. But last night out on the water setting the nets, for a moment that only lasted a moment, I knew who

I was, long ago. I was a kid, a brown boy with salt encrusted hair, dirty shorts or sarong and no shirt. I worked the rivers or the inlets, poling through the shallows in a little wooden boat or raft. And that was it. That's who I was once.

We rowed back to the beginning of the net, where it was secured by a stake pushed into the sand. Salt held the cork line out of the water.

'Hold this.'

I took the cork line. I could feel the fish hitting it – a sharp tug like when they take a hook. Then a lighter flurry as they struggle against the mesh. So I knew there would be a few.

Even when the sun or stars blaze, there is a moody stillness to this place. The country appears to offer up her secrets, the sea breaks the bar to flush the inlet, four-wheel drive tracks tether the country and yet somehow, she doesn't give much away. Lightning storms hang on the horizon for days, illuminating the strange cliffs and ghostly paperbarks, the silver and olive hues of the water ringed with emerald samphire swamps. It is often windy and still at once. There are secret corners where silence is shadowed by the roaring swell, the swell that throws up lumbering, dead monsters.

'Get up. You gotta see this,' Salt told me the next morning. 'There's something in the water.'

I sat up, swag and all. 'Is it five yet?'

'Close enough.' He was standing by the shore of the inlet.

The light flared from my mobile phone. 'It's fucking four twenty-seven!' I flopped back down into the sand and grumpily tried to justify half an hour's more sleep against some natural phenomenon.

I sat up again.

Salt stood on the edges of the water and strange blue lights shot out of his toes. Hot blue bullets rocketed away from his legs.

'Fire in the water.'

Every step as we pushed out the boat created a fiery turbulence. Every stroke of the oars made a sparkling rush in the inky brine and the dripping airborne oars traced wild arcs of colour beside the boat. Shrimp became tracer bullets.

Standing in the starlit dark with the moon gone and a white glow on the eastern horizon, the place made me feel like I'd crossed beyond an earthly threshold, with those surreal water lights and discovering my other life as a river boy. The wind had ceased its harrying but still the swell thumped outside the bar. Fish torpedoed away from our boat leaving comet tails of phosphorescence in their wake. Salt rowed and rowed, straight past the stake holding fast the net and out into the centre of the inlet and none of us dreaming folk even noticed.

'There won't be many fish,' he said of the nets. 'Fire in the water will light it up like Disneyland.'

Every mesh was illuminated, diamond lines of fishing net swooping down into an undersea glittery fantasia. We caught some yes, a few fat skippy and some mullet. The sky began to lighten and then all the fire faeries ran away … and after we picked the phosphorescent nets from out of the inlet, I ran with Stormboy along a deep, wild beach and when we got to the whale's skull, I told him about the brown boy.

DAMN THE BANKS

'Go in a bit.'

I am on the tiller, trying to creep the boat along the northern edge of the weed bank in Oyster Harbour; slow enough so Salt doesn't get tangled up in net, fast enough so the afternoon wind won't blow us onto the bank where we will get bogged. Salt likes to set his nets right along the edge, where the fish swim off during the withdrawing tide.

On the move across open water out to the banks, Salt stands amidships, looking ahead. He captains the tinny to me at the tiller with little left and right flicks of his fingers, whirling them to mean 'slow down' or 'throttle it'. When our positions are reversed I've tried these hand movements just to piss him off but somehow I never seem to do it right.

When Salt is playing out net, his hands are busy. He has to *mutter* directions, until I yell, 'What?' This system works fine at sea but on the banks ... well, we argue a lot. I find the whole setting-nets-on-the-banks thing rather stressful. Salt has to get the net positioned just right, so he catches lots of fish and maintains the legend. I don't want to get stuck. There are kids at home, dinner to cook and fading light.

Fishermen of the inlets and bays regard the water as 'grounds', much the same way a grazier observes their pasture. There is 'good bottom', 'weedy bottom' or 'sandy bottom'. Then there are the banks. A practised eye can see a weed or sandbank beneath the water by watching the ripples of wind on the surface.

'Out a bit.'

'Keep her to starboard at the north end of the bank.'

'Okay, she's on the bank. Out a bit.'

'Just follow it round to the Kalgan Stake.'

Oyster Harbour, like many south coast inlets, is delineated by a series of markers, improvised by commercial fishermen to show the edges of the banks. It takes no Nostradamus to predict that when planing along nicely and you pass a wooden stake in the water, then in a few seconds the bow will plough into a submerged sandbar and the whole boatload of people and gear will get thrown to forehead. At Irwin's Inlet the stakes are slender lengths of tea-tree bleached by salt and wind with white plastic reflectors or Emu Bitter cans nailed to them. Oyster Harbour has the Kalgan Stake, the Stick and the Periscope – a length of plumber's poly pipe with an elbow at the top.

'Follow it round to the Kalgan Stake but stay out of the weed. Don't wanna get any more o' that shit in the motor,' says Salt.

'Where's the Kalgan Stake?'

'Ahead.'

'That's a rock.'

'No, it's the Stake,' he says.

'It's a rock. It's that aggregate you told me about, where bream breed. If I go that way, I'll get bogged.'

'So, your eyes are better than mine. So, it's a rock. Where's the Stake? Stop. Stop. Stop!' He has a tangle of nets in his fist and more about his ankles.

'I can't! The wind is blowing me onto the bank.' And I'll get bogged.

I must be a bit of a pain in the arse, I think. I'm like a whingeing kid out here on the banks. But being bogged in a following wind really sucks.

Finally Salt throws out the last buoy. I breathe a sigh and turn away from the dreaded bank.

'Okay, we'll set the other net on the bank around from the Periscope.' He looks out over the bank. 'You can get across that one I reckon.'

I shake my head, appalled. The last time he told me this, I fell for it and got bogged right in the middle. It's not nice roaring into the centre of a weed bank on a dropping tide and seeing the tips of seagrass appear above the skin of the water, like the eyes of a thousand crocodiles. I love the water but pushing a seventeen-foot boat, laden with nets, through cobbler-infested seagrass in the half-light is not my idea of a good time.

The smell of cooking dinners floats across the water. I pray for a dropping wind and head for the channel as the sun goes down.

AND THEN THEY TALKED
ABOUT THE CRABS

After the eighty-odd kilometres through cow flats and karris I pulled into the parking spot at Irwin Inlet where fishers launch their boats and I groaned a little – not at the black swans or the glass-off silver waters but the expanse of weed poking through the inlet's skin all the way out to the island. Hard work getting a boat in and out of that.

I drove on to the shack at Foul Bay. The fisherman who owns the salmon lease there lets other commercial fishers stay there while working Irwin's. Bullet had already moved in his swag. He is a tidy soul. He picks up plastic rubbish wherever he goes. His esky sat on the sink. I peeked inside at his fare: a bag of lettuce, the carcass of a half-eaten cooked chook, some cheese and some cans of ginger beer, all swilling in melting ice. On the shack's veranda he'd piled some firewood for the Metters, his rubbish collection, an axe and his catching net.

Salt had left his caravan by the water tank. His outside light was on. When he arrived from town we took the boat out to the inlet, pushed her over the muddy flats that reached nearly to the island, then dropped the motor and fired her up. As we began planing I saw the other fishermen emerge from the rivers and the inlet mouth, they came from all their hidden places.

Commercial fishing in the estuaries of West Australia is beset by all sorts of laws, one of which is that the fishers shall only set nets one and a half hours before sunset. They also must have all of their gear out of the water by two hours after dawn (Perth time). These laws are supposed to reduce friction between commercials and amateurs and regulate the amount of fish taken.

At about three thirty in the afternoon the inlet was buzzing with small tinnies loaded down with nets. I could see Bullet's red jacket on the east side and Nails' neon green bending over the gunwales of his little blue ply boat near Possum Point. We set nets on the whiting banks and then motored down the causeway marked with the trunks of old tea-tree.

The causeways are important. Nobody sets nets across them, or if they do and someone runs into them and chops them up, they have to cop it sweet. They are the only safe passage in an inlet otherwise crisscrossed with net in the early evening.

On the way back to the parking spot, Nails beckoned Salt over. He explained, as the wind blew up, the boats clanking together, exactly where his nets were. They'd been to a Fisheries meeting a few hours before in town, so they debriefed about that. Then they talked about the crabs.

'Where's Jordie? I thought he'd be here this arvo,' I said.

Nails looked at Salt. 'Jordie's having some time off. Till his hands heal.'

Bullet came back to the shack half an hour after us. We lit the fire and cooked some dinner. He and Salt went over the meeting. He's a political animal, just like Salt. They'd both walked out fuming so there was a bit of ground to cover. Then they talked about the crabs.

'They're a fucking plague, mate,' said Bullet. 'I've never seen anything like it. I was unmeshin' crabs all day on Tuesday.'

At dawn, Salt and I waded, using sticks to guide the fish boxes over the water, to where we'd anchored the boat out near the island. Bullet took the Foul Bay way, along the beach to the inlet mouth and launched his boat into the white sands of the kelpy two waters.

We caught some lovely sea mullet and skippy in the first net. Most of them had their tails or guts chewed out by crabs but that is where a good filleting knife comes in. We were feeling pretty clever about avoiding those dastardly crabs.

On the second net, bigger mesh, deeper water, Salt and I realised we were in trouble. We had another fifteen minutes to get a few hundred metres of net out of the water and they were inundated with crabs. Each one takes an age to get out of the monofilament. So we decided to pick the whole lot up and unmesh them back at the shack. We hauled the net over the gunwale and it clanked, a heavy chain, of crustaceans.

And cobbler! Cobbler came up angry and poisonous with all their tri-spikes out to get us, their eel tails flickering against the nylon. Their treatment is never romantic – a fleshy thud of a waddy (or the 'priest': administrator of a cobbler's last rites) against the aluminium thwart. There is no other way to get them out of the nets.

It just got worse and worse. The only saving grace for us was that all the crabs were oversized. Undersized and they would have to have been unmeshed out on the water.

By then the pelicans had given up their scabbing and wandered off. We had to get the boat, overburdened with wet net, crabs, cobbler and boxes of mullet and bream, back over the shallow sandbank to the car park, so we could load the whole lot and take it back to camp. We got out and pushed. At one stage, Salt fell over into what he calls a 'swan hole', where the swans dig for worms. He filled up his waders but got to his feet pretty quickly when he thought about those crabs. 'Like fleas on a dog they are. Don't fall overboard, cos they'll *get ya!*'

We spent five hours getting the crabs and cobbler out of the net, as the swell at Foul Bay got bigger and bigger. Cobbler venom worked its way into every fish spine and crab bite in my hands, making me ache and swear and bitch.

Both Salt and I worried about Bullet stuck up at the bar by the swell. Once an hour I took a break to make us a cup of coffee. Individually we went down to the beach to look along the stormy shores for his car. Neither of us had eaten anything and it was two o'clock.

Finally Bullet turned up. He'd left his boat at the bar and chanced the four-wheel drive along the beach where the lowering tide was still smashing into the sand dune.

'Thought my job was done for the day,' he said, jumping into the boat to grab some net and help us with the crabs. 'Obviously not! Hey, at least these guys are a good size. Last week, Nails said all the ones he was catchin' were smaller than his dick.'

' ... !' (That was me.)

'Yeah fuck those crabs. They're bloody everywhere. They're plaguin'. Told yer, didn't I. Gotta do it yerself to find out, I know. But didn't I tell yer?'

I decided to have a week off, till my hands healed.

FISH HEAD

The kids at the boat ramp at Princess Royal Harbour eyed off the little rowboat tenders, upturned on the grass by the yacht club. I reckon ten minutes without anyone watching and those boys would have been rowing off into the nasty sou'-westerly, drunk on Red Bull and freedom, blown over to Possession Point without a hope of dinner.

They were fishing at the little service jetty. A sleepy Pacific gull cruised around them and a pelican lurked nearby. Salt was already there when I pulled into the car park. He had the tinny and trailer waiting on the ramp. The boys thought he was great – a real old salt – someone who could take a bit of lip and give some back.

'You won't catch any fish here,' said Salt. 'Too shallow.'

'We just caught a skippy.'

'What ya using for bait then?'

One of the boys, the skinny black jeans, black shirt, older than the other, plumper kids, toed something lying on the concrete. 'Mullet.'

Salt stepped a little closer. The mullet was little more than a head with some meat attached. The head was huge. The whole fish would have been the size of a salmon. I knew where that mullet came from just by looking at it. So did Salt.

'Where'd you get that mullet?'

'Me mate's freezer.'

'Oh. Yeah ... ah, where'd he get it?'

'The mullet? He's got a shitload in his freezer.'

'Where'd he get 'em?'

'It's his dad's freezer.'

'Mmm?'

'I think his uncle got them.'

'His uncle. Who's his uncle?'

'Dunno. His uncle just went out and got them.'

'Yeah, *but where'd he get them*?'

The kid was looking at the fish head now. Then he looked at me and at Salt and then back to me.

'Salt really likes Mullet,' I said.

On Salt's advice, one of the boys stuffed the mullet head into an empty corn chips bag so the pelican wouldn't grab it. He was right, the pelicans *were* edging closer every time the kids moved away. They wrapped up the fish head and looked to Salt for approval. He nodded.

They helped us untie the ropes and push out the boat.

'That was a bloody Pallinup mullet,' Salt growled as we chugged away. 'Skippy bait, for crying out loud.'

We returned four hours later. The boys had jumped the gates into the marina (or charmed their way in) and were fishing in the deep, out by the port light, as the sun went down. One figure waved and I saw the silver glint of the chip bag in his hand.

TONIGHT

Tonight we worked under the lamp in our special flathead spot. I've been fishing with Salt for five years now and the seasonal swarm of flathead into the harbour still amazes me. A month ago we picked up a few flathead in Oyster Harbour.

Salt said, 'They got roe in 'em?'

'Yep.'

'They're early. Everything's early this year. Let's get out there before the seal finds us.'

He was speaking of the seal who, once he understands where we are setting, will treat our nets like the seafood section of the supermarket. All he wants is the flathead livers but he destroys all flesh in his mission. We can't set in the same spot again for months.

The flathead were early like the plum tree flowers and the black king skinks emerging from their winter dens. I could smell pink jasmine flowers, travelling to me like sure mail across the water.

Tonight, on a rough sea, we gathered a lovely box of flathead and travelled home through the channel, where the incoming tide hit the westerly wind wave of the inlet, past the steaming heaps of woodchips, the chugging train, the trucks, the Chinese freighter, the crew on deck in overalls and hard hats, smoking cigarettes under orange lights, under the seven-metre sign: SAFETY + FIRST.

The wind dropped. The seal hadn't found us. I could smell

the clear cedar of the woodchips. The sea glassed over and, all across the harbour, navigation lights raced in bright streaks towards us, drowning out the sound of the two-stroke.

LEGENDS

Sometimes I'll see them in a boat or sitting at a kitchen table or worrying crabs out of nets and I can hardly believe these south coast fishers are real and not from a romantic painting, centuries old. But they can wield a mobile phone as easily as sling new net. Some use the internet to check the weather or the fish prices on their laptops wherever they get into range. Behind their success and survival is always a wily humour, an old, clannish wisdom, a strong body, a keen sense of natural history and a knowledge of their place in the world.

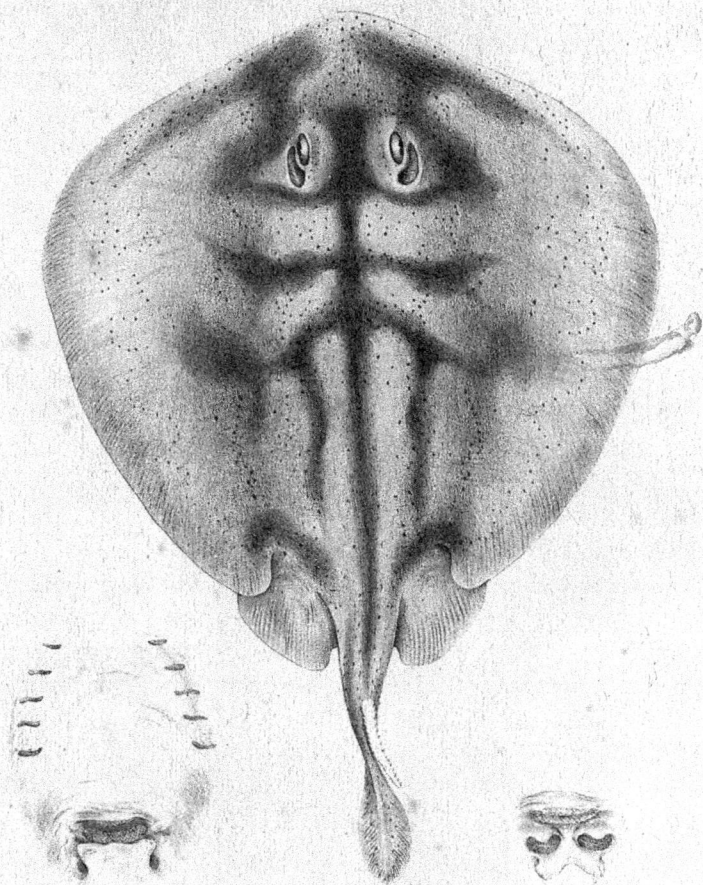

JOLLY AND HIS BOY

'I think I've got whiting fever,' said Salt after pulling some small brown specimens from Oyster Harbour. Someone said there were King George whiting at Casey's Beach, and they are always bigger and whiter out there, cleaner fish from the deep clear waters, not like the inlet fish.

We set nets in the channel between Michaelmas Island and the bleached sands of the opposite shore. Then we sat around, watching the sun go down, drinking coffee from the plastic thermos.

A tinny thudded towards us. 'What's his number?' Salt asked.

'Can't see. Oh, it's Jolly Roger and his son.'

Jolly pulled in alongside us. 'Where'd you set?'

Salt showed him a squiggle of fingers, which all fisherfolk except me seem to understand, and Jolly took off to set his nets somewhere else, the boy a lean figurehead on the bow. He returned twenty minutes later and eased into our gunwale, killed the motor and cracked a stubby.

'You won't be having a coffee then,' I said.

'Nah mate, that stuff'll kill ya.'

Jolly wore waders and a filthy old jumper. Salt wore waders and a filthy old jumper. Jolly must be forty years younger than Salt but both of them possess a kind of corpulent anarchism that is out of date in any land-based society and yet is strangely graceful at sea.

His son grabbed the beam of both boats to stop them clashing. He was about nine and keen as a kelpie. Whilst Salt and Jolly swapped anecdotes and expletives regarding the dubious parentage of the new marine safety officer, Jolly's boy and I chatted.

'You don't get seasick then?'

He shook his head. 'Nah. Never!'

He told me about the pre-dawn mornings when his dad heads out to the whiting grounds. The boy sleeps in the bow. He pointed to his nest of life jackets and hessian sacks. 'Nice and warm. Anyway, it's boring when Dad's setting nets. He wakes me up when it's time to pick up. That's good.'

He swept the seaweed off the deck, while the net was out, to the approving nod of his father and then looked around for another job.

Jolly's sixteen-foot aluminium boat is standard issue for most south-west inshore fishers. Thanks to the new marine safety officer's crackdown on commercial vessels, the foredeck was festooned with fire-extinguishers, EPIRBs and sodden flares, along with more essential items such as a gaff, catching net, squid jigs, torch, jump starter, red bucket, spare bricks for net anchors, buoys, rotten pilchards, Danforth anchor, fluorescent lights, trolling lures, spare rowlock, pliers, spark plug puller and a sixpack of beer.

His boat was tidy enough, despite all this. The working deck, an area of one or two squares, is where the nets are played out, hauled in and fish unmeshed. A lot of these boats have a waist-high rail around the sides, to save us from going over in a swell – a rail I've been very grateful for three or four times now.

Eventually it was dark enough for us to pick up the nets. The air was thick and greasy, with no wind, and the sea heaved up a big, gentle swell. We pulled nets out of the deep, black water in the channel between the mainland and the island, looking over occasionally to see Jolly Roger and his son doing the same under the blue glow of the fluorescent light.

A GUY THING

We hurled crab pots into clear patches skirted with weed. Early the next morning we flew across the harbour on a strange high tide to pick them up.

Crabs love eating trumpeters and this is a good thing, seeing the trumpeters are a spiny, orchestral nuisance in the nets. So we returned to land with a box full of blue mannas bouncing in the bow. At the boat ramp, Salt told me with a nasty grin that he was going to try driving the boat onto the trailer, rather than winching it up, 'Just because I never done it before.'

'Can't we just winch it? It's too windy.'

But he handed me the keys and I climbed out of the boat and stepped *very* carefully across the slimy jetty timbers, heading for the car park.

I reversed the trailer down the boat ramp and stood in position at the winch. Salt churned towards the trailer and I could see the wind blowing the bow over too far. My job here was like being the flunky when bleeding brakes or helping husband reverse a caravan into a ditch. I was going to get yelled at. Or I was going to yell. Or, I was going to just walk away and make a nice cup of tea. Given the lack of a kettle, the first two scenarios were most likely.

Salt roared in, missed the rollers by an inch or so and drove the boat nearly up to the winch in his enthusiasm. I waded in, pushed the Westerberg off and we went again.

I was knee-deep and sounding by this stage. Suddenly I realised there were two handsome men standing behind me.

'Do you need some help?'

I looked to the uniform. Grey vest over grey shirt over grey trousers. Both men had haircuts like US marines but their faces were more like outdoorsy cops. Department of Fisheries. Oh.

Salt aimed at the trailer again. It's a *thing* you know, a *guy thing*. Why can't we give up and winch her on? Well, not any more because some other blokes are watching.

'How's it going, Salt?' one of the officers yelled.

It threw him off. I pushed the boat off the wheel guards and we tried again.

Salt drove her on nice and straight the third time, making us both look good as I clanked the ratchet and clinched her to the trailer. I drove up the ramp, the Fisheries officers walking alongside the boat, Salt standing amidships, looking ahead.

In the car park I watched the wonders of Fisheries and fishermen at work.

'What are you catching today, Salt? Crabs, hey.' Brad started poking through the box, looking for undersized ones. (Ever tried to 'poke through' a box of live crabs?)

'Yeah, well. It's pretty heavy. You wanna lift it into the ute for me?'

'Sure, mate.' He struggled to get the box under the rail and nodded at his colleague to help him. 'I hear you've been out at Irwin Inlet.'

'Who told you that?'

'Grievous. He's been sending snapper and cobbler up to Perth. What did you get out there?'

'Ohh, I dunno. We got ... what'd we get Sarah? A box?'

I nodded, five times.

'Who else was out there when you were there, Salt?'

'Nails. Saw him once ... hey, where did Grievous get that snapper?'

'Wilson's. The bar opened three days ago.'

'Have you heard what they're gettin' down at Pallinup?' Salt asked.

'Oh, it's all quietened down a bit now.'

'Yeah, heard about the mullet dropping off. Musta been poached. Hung any poachers lately?'

Officers and commercials in the same car park together have a small amount of protocol to perform before they get down to the real business of the day, the gossip. But it doesn't always flow both ways. I think Salt left with more information that day, and saved his back too.

HIS DAD

I watched the weathervane spin on its bamboo stake in the wind. I watched it turn to the north and then change its mind, again and again.

Salt rang. 'Whaddaya reckon?'

'It's a bit strange.'

'Blowing its guts out on this side of town. The BOM says it'll turn sou'-west and then things may get interesting. Tell yer what. I'll ring in another hour.'

Shark rang. 'Can't come over to fix your computer/ download stuff/drink copious cups of tea. Dylan's here and we're going down to the White Star for a drink. Do you want to come down?'

'Mmm. Can I get back to you on that one?'

'We won't be there long. Just a quick drink.'

Dylan. Pub. Just a quick drink. Those three elements only work together when there is a bouncer involved. Salt rang back, uncanny in his ability to sniff out that I might be considering other options.

'Ah, bugger it,' he said. 'Let's go.'

We set some net out near Mistaken Island. Salt played the mesh out over the stern and I drove the dinghy. The early evening gleamed sulphurous yellow. The sou'-westerly began to freshen. Huge swells rolled in from the east, still coming in from the big blow a few days before. It felt all wrong. We were both jittery: me because I didn't know what the weather was about to do – and Salt, because he did.

'We shouldn't be out here, by rights.'

'Yeah, thanks Salt. That's great.' I motored up another mountain that kept getting pushed taller by the wind hitting the swell. I noticed that no other boats were in the Sound. Even Grievous had stayed home.

'How's about we untie this net halfway and chuck a buoy on it?'

'Good idea.' That meant about seven hundred metres less of net to deal with when the storm hit.

'And then we'll start picking up the first net, as soon as we're done here.'

'Good-oh.'

A shark meandered past the bow, its charcoal-lined fin slicing through the chop, sluicing a little eddy in its wake. We finished the net and motored in circles out by Johnno's mussel lease, avoiding the ropes that held the buoys together, watching the horizon.

A mussel buoy bobbed, hairy with algae and weed. Most of the buoys were oblong-shaped but this one was round and bobbing just above the water, its hairy skull revealed and then cloaked beneath the next wave.

'Looks like my old man's head,' said Salt.

My mind was off with the horizon, with the brewing storm, and with Dylan and Shark at the pub. I nearly missed what Salt said. But something in the sound of his voice called me back.

'What did you say?'

'That buoy looks like my old man's head. When I found him.'

Salt was sharking at Cape Riche when he got the call that his father was missing. They'd found his boat washed up on the banks at Floodgates, nets stowed neat, the red dog waiting on deck, alone.

Salt found his body, after three days of searching with his brothers and police divers, in the river that flows from the

Torbay Inlet to the sea. The fisherman of incredible strength, that one-armed poacher of legend, had come fatally unstuck.

Salt Senior rowed a wooden boat by way of bolting the oars together. He built a shack on Muttonbird Island. He used to pull salmon nets in with one arm and one leg. He had so many fishing camps up and down the coast that he buried food stashes at each one.

There are generations of drowners in this town and stories of ancestors mistaken for seals and shot dead, men who lived on islands and the women who grew up their babies and fished alongside their husbands. No wonder people of Salt's ilk struggle to make sense of the rules these days. He used to chuck a match into the scrub when the wind was right, to rid the dry autumn bush of ticks and keep the kangaroos happy with fresh new shoots. His family camped for weeks round the smouldering stump of a long-dead yate tree by Wilson Inlet, netting bream, fat, oily mullet and those big grunters, the mulloway. If they needed to drive a truck on the beach to save their backs from hauling tons of salmon over the sand dunes, they built themselves a road with mattocks and axes.

Salt Senior's was a mysterious end, shared and seen by no one. Yet this end is experienced in the ropey, briny dreams of fishermen everywhere: the treacle swim, the crystalline sound of undersea bubbles and the waves talking to the tinny above.

'The best way to go,' said Salt.

The sound of his voice that day out on the water, with my whole being wanting to be somewhere else, put things back into perspective for me. I stopped my yearning for the relative sanity of Dylan and Shark and red wine near the fireplace at the pub and ceased worrying about what would or wouldn't happen with the weather. It's like getting tattooed, I reasoned to myself. There's no point going through it twice.

So we picked up the nets early and happened across a nice school of rainbow leatherjackets. The storm gathered momentum as we charged into the wind across the Sound, the boat laden with fish and nets. I was soaked to my flesh by the bow wave hurled up in my face by the nasty sou'-westerly but also soaked with a sense of occasion and comfortable with my own mortality. The channel lights beckoned us safely home.

THE FLATHEAD PATCH

According to Salt, Grievous is the Dark Overlord of the Inlets. I don't really know when The Flathead Wars began. Possibly both their fathers barneyed over flathead too.

When working with Salt, my experiences with Grievous tend to be profoundly negative but if I branch away from Salt's company, I've always found him pretty much okay. Recently I asked Grievous if I could include him in this book. He knows I work for Salt and yet he grinned and said, 'Yeah, sure Sarah.' He went on to tell me about his old man who sailed everywhere in his wooden carvel complete with grasstree-tarred sails, eschewing outboard motors. Grievous seemed happy that someone, even if it was the lowly deckie of his nemesis, was documenting the heritage.

Last year Salt and I rediscovered the spot near the channel heads where flathead gather for their mysterious conferences. We started netting there for the Sunday seafood markets. So did Grievous.

Salt played out nets from the pile on the deck and I kept the boat throttled into the wind, trying to keep her straight. I manoeuvred her from the channel marker and headed for the yellow hazard beacon. A few metres to the east waves sloshed over the little reef.

Salt had pulled over only the first length of net off the boat in his backyard to straighten out any tangles, so the rest of the net was a mess of sticks and weed. He fiddled about with all the knots and rolled up tangles, saying, 'Stop. Stop.' The boat blew off course and towards the rocky headland. That didn't bother Salt. 'More fish over there anyway,' he said but I steered back for the marker, so that by the time we were done the net ran in big zigzags through the flathead patch. Digger sat on the thwart and watched us. Salt chucked the last buoy into the sea. I headed for calmer waters, somewhere out of the wind, to wait for sunset.

We watched Grievous roar across the harbour. He stood at the tiller, at the stern of the boat, holding a rope tied to the bow. Going with the wind, he churned towards the little reef where we'd thrown out the first buoy.

'What's he doing?'

'I dunno. Did he have some leatherie pots there?'

Grievous slowed down and then turned into the channel. He stopped. He was too far away for me to see much of what he was doing but I did see him throw something over.

'He's doin' something. What the fuck is he doin'?'

Whenever Grievous is in the same waters, I get a running commentary from Salt. This knowledgeable rant is largely anticipation and changes direction as many times as Grievous does in his boat. 'He's gonna put in some pots. Then he'll head over the south side and set some nets there. No. He'll put some pots in the south side ...'

We drank some coffee, watching the figure of Grievous move about in his tinny and chuck things into the water. As it darkened the wind also stiffened and the tide started going out, creating strong currents near the channel. I set up the light and mucked about with the jump starter until I had the fluorescent light flickering above me. Then we motored back to the first buoy. Grievous had disappeared into the Sound.

It is a distinctive feel in the rope when another fisher sets nets over the top of the one being hauled. It grinds against the other net, a different feel to pulling up ancient grapple irons or thrashing stingrays. 'Got an anchor there?' Salt said to me. I'd been doing the hauling lately because his shoulder was playing up. I didn't say anything. I knew it wasn't an old anchor. It was Grievous' net.

The night had set in but the light illuminated the bright green net running over the top of Salt's old brown one as it surfaced. Digger leaned over the gunwale, interested.

Salt started going postal. We had to pull Grievous' net over the top of the boat and then ours underneath. A big ask on a gathering wind. But it was the slight to his dignity, his territorialism and his fishy paternalism that bothered Salt the most. He pulled out his filleting knife. 'If he's done it again, I'll cut the fucker up.'

Over the noise of the wind and the slop around the reef, I heard Grievous' outboard.

'Come and get yer fucking net!' Salt pulled Grievous' net out of the water and started tearing holes in it.

A red flathead wriggled in the piece of Grievous' net that I held. I taxed it, laughing, and chucked it in the box. First fish for the night and it was Grievous'. Brilliant! Then I started pulling his net over the deck, over the outboard and the fluorescent light, over the bow where, of course, it caught on everything. Salt was so busy ripping holes in monofilament and glaring out to sea that he wasn't much help.

At the channel, Grievous started picking up, his motor running. He worked his way toward us quickly, chucking the net on the deck, fish and all. He was closer a few minutes later, then closer. I knew this meant our nets would cross again.

They did. The shouting intensified.

'You're a fucking dickhead, Salt.'

'What'd he say?'

'Dunno,' I muttered. I pulled the second transgression out of the water.

'Don't pull that one over the boat. Make him come and get it. COME AND GET YER FUCKING NET.'

'You've got a short memory, Salt,' Grievous screamed into the wind, his voice pitched high. 'You've got one buoy at the reef and the other over there,' he pointed to the marker. 'So what the fuck is the middle of your net doin' all the way over here?'

'What's that bastard sayin'?'

Digger saw Grievous' boat coming towards his perch on the bow. It must have seemed like a shouting white light to the dog. He started up a panicked barking, slipped on the wet aluminium and fell overboard into the sea.

Great – black water, the night getting blacker and a bull-mastiff floundering through two fishing nets. I gave both cork lines to Salt and started hunting around for a torch.

'You're a fucking dickhead,' Grievous shouted again. 'Don't you remember the last meeting about this shit? If you zigzag yer nets, put a buoy on the *outside*.'

I couldn't see the dog anywhere.

'What'd he say? I'M NOT LISTENIN' TO A PIECE O' SHIT LIKE YOU.'

Digger swam into the circle of light and struggled towards the gunwale. I hauled him over the side by the scruff of his neck.

Then Grievous got to our boat, his wet-weather gear shiny with spray, a lean man, wizened for his age. 'If you zigzag yer nets, put a buoy on the outside. That's what we worked out last year.'

'What *outside*? What's the *outside* of a net?'

'You're not a fisherman if you don't know that.'

'*You're* not a fucking fisherman.'

The two fishermen glared at each other.

The gunwales of both boats began to clang against each other. Grievous' propeller was heading for Salt's net.

'Don't you run over my net,' Salt warned him.

'Whaddya gonna do about it?' Grievous fronted him, leaving the motor in forward gear.

'Just drop the net, Salt,' I said. I knew it would then sink and go under. Salt was hanging on to his net so tight it was pulling the two fishermen together. Grievous was doing the same with his. As soon as both men dropped their nets we were able to go our separate ways, the dog shaking the sea off himself.

We continued picking up, and Grievous' fluorescent light and his chugging outboard retreated into the night.

Salt said, 'At least we're talking again.'

Grievous and Salt's next conversation was twelve months later in exactly the same place and over the same crossed nets. This time Grievous had his own deckie, who sat quietly in the boat when Salt pulled out his filleting knife. I was so shocked by the open display of knives and oars that I shut up too. So both us deckies sat like slapped kewpie dolls while the two fishermen raged and spat at each other.

This season, we arrived late one night to the reef to find Grievous' buoys in the water and him nowhere to be seen.

'We'll set here anyway,' Salt began pulling the tarp off the nets.

'Don't. We could just head outside and set for whiting. Too much trouble.' There was no way I wanted to be in the wrong at that time of night. Being vaguely in the right was bad enough.

'Fuck it. Let him get a taste.'

With control of the tiller, I was able to keep the net away from Grievous', hoping he hadn't set in a zigzag. Salt nagged at me to get closer. It was all rather stressful. Under harassment from me, we picked up early and got out of there before Grievous returned.

One flathead.

I hoped that result would signify the end of the affair but it doesn't seem to work like that with fishermen. Salt keeps worrying at the issue like a bit player in a Greek drama. Grievous maintains a wily silence.

And so on they go. The Flathead Wars.

PRINCESS ROYAL PRICK

Salt and I went out to throw crab pots into the shallows of the harbour on a Thursday. I baited them with trumpeters caught from the previous night's flathead shot. We drifted about, looking for patches of sand and healthy seagrass. Over the past decade the seagrass has been struggling against the march of an invasive algae that Salt calls 'carpet', 'snotweed' or 'shit'.

On the Friday we went around, rebaiting the pots and checking the catch, leaving the crabs in the pots so they would be alive for the markets. At this time of year, the females are 'berried', their bellies laden with a mass of eggs that looks like dirty foam rubber. It's always a joy for me to throw back those expectant mothers, to participate in maintaining the abundance.

Grievous set his pots that night in the Gilgie Holes, a section of the harbour divided from the rest by a massive sandbar. We often see him out there at dawn, unmeshing skippy, cobbler and salmon trout, bending over the gunwales with a swarm of pelicans around him.

On Saturday we moved around the shallows between the buoys, pulling pots. Every single crab was gone. The pots were turned over or moved from their sandy spot to the 'carpet'. Bait, elastic – gone. Even a whole pot was missing.

It happens often but usually in a more haphazard manner. Some opportunists just can't help themselves. Salt is generous then – more so than I. 'Well, at least someone had a good feed,' he says. This day was different. Every pot pulled was met with his silence that grew more ominous, the pots sitting dripping on the rails of the boat as we stared at the emptiness, and then came a series of appalled expletives.

This was a concentrated hit, an operation. Even the berried females were gone. The sinking feeling I got looking at those empty pots made the redneck in me shuffle from her porch (the creak of the floorboards and that sure snap of the bolt going home on the rifle). I wanted to write on some plastic tags and attach them to the pots: 'Look behind you, ARSEHOLE'. Of course it was all too late by then.

As Salt and Grievous don't talk to each other unless they are brawling, Mrs Grievous approached me at the Sunday markets.

'Did Salt get his pots done over on Friday night?'

The Oyster Boys overheard. 'Ahh yes, they were lovely crabs, thanks,' giggled Kilpatrick.

'Grievous and his brother had their pots ratted too,' she said.

'Mmm. Those ones were tasty too,' said Gawain.

Seventy-five pots was a busy night for the crab thief and would have made a quick grand or two in Perth. The Oyster Boys were pragmatic. Gawain sets leatherjacket pots in the Sound and they get regularly vandalised and pilfered. 'You just gotta get them up,' he told me. 'You can't leave crabs or fish in there, it's open slather.'

Grievous got into the habit of writing down plate numbers of cars at the boat ramp late at night. Salt rang Fisheries. Mrs Grievous wanted to call the police. I just wanted to catch the crab thief in the act and ask them to explain the loaded shotgun in my hands. Prick.

SUPER FISHERIES OFFICER GUY

I was quite excited about getting the Fisheries involved to catch the crab thief, seeing as yours truly harbours a guilty lust for Fisheries officers. Guilty, because the Department of Fisheries and commercial fishers are the Montague and Capulet families of the ocean. Lust, because Fisheries officers are such a damn sexy bunch that every time they appear in uniform at the boat ramp, something strange happens to me. I get flustered, forget things, like how to speak, and deeply regret my choice of attire. The fact that the tinny workplace requires a raincoat and plastic pants has no bearing on my desire to be wearing something more attractive when these strapping lads come calling.

Salt: 'Sarah, have you met Brad?'

Brad is tall, impossibly handsome and lucky enough to have a job that requires a really cool uniform. No plastic pants for him. He wears silver cargo pants and a silver padded vest with strategic quilting seams to create an impressive sixpack. Uniform designers were thinking Superhero of the Sea when they stitched up this contract for the Fisheries Department. Brad has that fit, outdoorsy look of someone who spends plenty of sea time that does not involve unmeshing flathead, thumping cobbler on the head or picking rotten starfish from nets. If he was American, Brad would have a name like Chuck or Hank. He even smells okay. Far out.

Me, waving flies from my fish gut–encrusted raincoat: 'Hi Brad.'

We were launching the dinghy one evening when a whole boatload of Fisheries came in. These guys were not the inspectors of the fisheries world but its special investigators. They were knocking off for the day and we were just going out.

'You after whiting tonight?'

Salt reversed the trailer down the ramp. I stood at the winch, a happy girl.

'No, flathead. What have you guys been up to today?'

One of them leaned out of his immaculately clean boat and gave me a blue-eyed smile. 'Gonad counts on herring.'

Phwoar ... 'Really? Gonad counts? Amazing.' (Giggle.)

'Have you seen any around lately?'

Gonads?

'No, haven't seen much herring.' Probably because they weren't really running at the time, but I didn't say that.

I wasn't really focussing on my job. I let the ratchet off the winch, forgetting that Salt had greased the roller the previous day. So the boat rolled straight off the trailer and into the sea, the cable still hooked to the bow, winch handle spinning wildly. Something you must never do – and usually do anyway in the heat of the moment – is attempt to stop a spinning winch handle with your own flesh and bone. The handle has the weight of a whole boat behind it. Don't do it.

I'm pretty sure I knocked a chip out of my thumb bone. My hand swelled into a rather useless appendage and I was left in a world of pain which intensified my confused feelings of embarrassment and grumpiness.

'I've never done that before,' I explained to Gonad Man, who was watching. My dog jumped into his boat.

'No, really, I haven't!'

This kind of protesting twice always makes things look worse. To compound it all, Digger refused to get out of the Department vessel. Gonads and all.

Recently Brad introduced his new colleague to us. They'd been out pulling Salt's crab pots so that Brad could show the newbie how they worked. Although this act was dressed up as altruism on behalf of the Department, it may have been an exercise in catching out Salt, not the crab thief. Of course I made this observation later, once my hormones had settled down.

Salt patted my shoulder with a slapping on plastic sound. 'Just as well my deckie didn't see you blokes pulling those pots,' he said. 'She can see them from her house. She's cleared all the trees from around her kitchen window and is holed up there all night with an arsenal: crossbows, shotguns. She's a pretty good shot too. She'd kill ya as soon as look at ya!'

GOOD FRIDAY

'Well if that's a Good Friday, I'd hate to see a Bad One.' Salt watched Fisheries drive away from the boat ramp.

On Thursday night we'd set nets and crab pots as normal, in anticipation of the Easter Sunday markets. As far as Salt was concerned, the Fisheries laws on public holidays worked the same as for Saturday – all gear out of the estuaries within two hours after dawn. The only problem so far with this Good Friday morning was the thunder and lightning.

The last time we fished during a lightning storm, it started off a gorgeous, balmy afternoon. Sure, the eastern skies were gunmetal grey but it was so hot and still that we didn't bother with wet-weather gear. I was wearing jeans and a t-shirt; Stormboy, even less. It was one of the rare times I got him out on the water; 'We're just going out to set a few nets. Back in an hour. C'mon, son.'

We motored out to the mussel farms over the glass-off and threw the first buoy overboard. I took care of the tiller, Stormboy sat amidships and Salt played out nets over the stern. A ripple played across the water.

'Wind'll be up in a moment,' said Salt.

Within five minutes lightning forked into the sea around us, forty-knot winds blew waves that only a gnarly nor'-easterly can throw up and the rain was hurting my face. I put the motor in neutral and we let the wind blow the boat over the water, no propulsion needed to play out the nets. It started hailing and soon I was picking icy stones from my hair the shape of glass shards and as big as my thumbnail. Salt held a fish box over his head and let go of the net. Stormboy covered himself with a tarp and sat huddled like an old plant. I stayed on the tiller, cowled in lengths of shade cloth. I couldn't make sense of where I was or even which direction we were heading in because visibility was only about five metres. During that squall, despite our mad laughter and lightning streaking into the sea, and bald, naked fear and hail hitting us like broke middies in a bar fight, not one of us said out loud, 'I'm a bit worried about being the highest point in the harbour and sitting in an aluminium boat.'

The storm roared through the inlet, through the channel and out into King George Sound. By the time we'd thrown out the last buoy, the sun shone again. We cruised into the jetty to see a shore red with gravel from the car park. A very dry Aboriginal family spilled out of their misted up van and ventured to the jetty with their rods to catch some black bream.

So, on Good Friday, the sheet lightning was a little easier to bear, bouncing harmlessly from cloud to cloud. But the nets were crammed with undersized crabs and the wind was blowing the boat off the nets. I had to pin it against the gunwale with one foot and unmesh angry crabs at the same time. You should try this one day. Go on.

The hail started and it got to the point where I could only laugh because my face was too numb to hurt. It took two hours to unmesh those crabs, so we were way over our welcome in the inlet. We still had to pick up the crab pots. I was beginning to suffer for lack of an early-morning coffee.

Finally, we pulled into the jetty. I saw the white ute parked beside Salt's. Oh nice ... Fisheries officers. Some eye candy on a morning devoid of any joy so far. Salt gave me the keys to his car. I welcomed them as I shuffled wetly off the jetty. They both looked at me strangely.

I wondered about that look as they stood, arms folded, waiting for me to get the boat up the ramp.

Then they proceeded to confiscate the whole catch, all the nets and all of the crab pots. The nets should have been out of the water before sunset *previous* to a public holiday. They arranged to interview Salt and gave him a summons for the magistrates court. Then they drove away, their ute groaning with booty.

PETTY SESSIONS

Salt made a show in court, for fishing illegally on Good Friday.

Sitting in the courthouse waiting room is always a condensed study of the human condition and this day there was even a bit of claret spilled (and some spitting). Everyone was summoned to appear at nine o'clock. Unfortunately on this day, sixty-three people were summoned to appear at nine o'clock and the room began to resemble the wild party that had brought most of them there in the first place.

Brad, resplendent in a suit and polished shoes instead of his usual Super Fisheries Officer Guy fatigues, came to sit with Salt, me and Kermit. Kermit had been nabbed for having his nets in the water too many hours after dawn. It's funny really. Brad as prosecutor should have been the enemy today but faced with the rest of the room, he was a kind of brother. There was still plenty of gossip to cover and Salt wanted to know a few things about the cockle market.

People hugged and chuckled babies. The Aboriginal liaison officer, a humorous woman, walked around talking everyone up. 'Well!' she shouted. 'It's good to see there's more men than women today. At least the girls have been behavin' themselves a bit better, hey.'

A young woman wearing several hoodies, stained white tights and black vinyl boots lurched around before finding a seat that overlooked the stairs. She seemed very much alone and just holding herself together. Mothers dressed like real estate agents ushered in their naughty daughters. A whole family wore black fedoras, sharp suits and smiles. A middle-aged man sat alone on the plywood chair, brooding. A couple of local bikies, sans colours, hung around the water fountain, chatting to a woman – black skirt, black jacket, black hat.

She walked past the waif in white tights, doubled back and sat down, too close. 'I know what you were thinking and I wouldn't, if I were you.'

White Tights laughed, too loud and unsteady. 'Ahh, haw ha! You got it. You knew what I was thinking.'

'Yeah. Don't ever think about trying to trip me up again.' She stayed in her seat and looked at White Tights, her eyes all glittery.

White Tights started squirming in her chair. 'I did not try to trip you up. I was thinking something else. How do you know what I was thinking? You don't know what I was thinking at all.'

People stopped talking.

'She tried to trip me up,' Black Hat said when the Aboriginal liaison officer raised her eyebrows.

'So what are you doing sitting next to her?' she retorted. 'Got your legal aid sorted?'

Black Hat stood. She must have been six foot tall and built like the proverbial. She looked at the clipboard. White Tights stood up and started calling her a bitch and said she so did not try to trip her up. Foam worked its way between the gaps in her teeth and settled into the corners of her mouth.

'Sit down darling,' Black Hat was in total control. She was even smiling. 'Go on, you know you can do it. You've obviously got some problems but you can sit down. Just bend your knees and put your arse on that chair.'

People tittered. White Tights sat down and Black Hat sat next to her again. The Noongar woman went away shaking her head.

I went downstairs to get some fresh air, and because Black Hat was cultivating an audience I didn't want to be part of. Outside I talked to the bikies who said they had been given incorrect move-on orders whilst drinking in one pub and been arrested at another. The Aboriginal liaison officer came outside and cadged a quick cigarette from the taller bikie, 'Before I gotta get back in there.'

Two young men, one bristling with an orange prickle haircut, came outside. 'You shoulda seen that shit. That crazy bitch started throwing punches at yer mate in the black hat!'

'No way!' Everyone started laughing.

'For crying out loud,' said the liaison officer. 'And I just told all the women in the room they were better behaved than men. I'll shut me trap next time.'

Salt's case was deemed by the magistrate as too time-consuming for a petty sessions hearing with sixty people waiting. She wanted to think about it some more. Kermit, representing himself, pulled out his doorstop of evidence and his packed lunch. She booted him out too. Adjourned until Friday.

Postscript: it was expensive.

Expensive for Salt anyway: when Fisheries took their original statement from Salt, they asked him why I was aboard on the offending morning, presumably in an attempt to charge me as well. It is on the official record that, according to Salt, I was carrying out my duty as a lightning rod.

YOUR FLARES ARE OUT OF DATE, SIR.

'Hi Chief. How are we today?'

As soon as someone in uniform approaches Salt on a jetty, I see him get antsy. That kind of pseudo-casual greeting usually signals the beginning and end of all pleasantries. Trevor is the new marine safety officer. He's new to town and has just met Salt for the first time. Poor guy.

'So ... I'm just checking that your boat meets all the current safety requirements.'

'No bastard's had to rescue me yet.'

'Do you have an EPIRB? Lifejackets? A gas horn? What about a fire-extinguisher?'

'We're just checking crab pots mate! Just over there.'

'We've got a bailer,' I pointed to the red plastic bucket in the bow. 'That's all we need right? We're in protected waters and we don't have an inboard motor.' I was right. I was so bloody right.

Trevor sighed and shook his head. 'This is a survey-exempt commercial vessel. Recreational maritime regulations are not applicable to survey-exempt commercial vessels.'

But I saw a little twitch when he said that, as though he were mentally fumbling for his absent clipboard. 'Are you sure about that?' I eyeballed him.

He wasn't sure and now I'd embarrassed him in front of Salt, his prize. It wouldn't be the last time we saw Trevor.

We returned to the jetty from setting the pots again a few days later and he was waiting for us, clutching a clipboard.

'He's been at me on the phone for days now,' Salt grumbled. 'I'm gonna swear at him, if he gives me a hard time.'

There are several kinds of residents at the boat ramp by the slipway. There's a pair of steel-capped boots that have been living there for quite a while now. There are some old men who sit in their cars all day, drinking beer, chatting through wound-down windows and looking out to sea. Then there are public officers. Trevor was eating lunch when he saw Salt motor up. Gold.

He waited patiently while Salt took a few runs at driving onto the trailer. Once she was winched and on dry ground, he started.

'So, Chief ...'

Salt started too, launching straight into combat mode. 'No I don't have your fucking EfuckingPIRBfirefuckingextinguisher ... but would you like to see my flares?'

Trevor took the flares and examined the expiry date. 'These are three years and two months old. Two months out of date.'

'They are guaranteed for six years.'

'The maritime safety regulations state –'

'I don't give a fuck mate. You've been doggin' me all week. I know who I'd feel *safety* with on a boat and it's not fucking you. I was fishin' before you were born, probly before yer dad was born. What's yer fucking problem?'

'I don't have a problem, *sir*.' Trevor leaned the clipboard on the deck to cross a box. His unbuttoned shirt flapped open to reveal the hairy bulge that held his lunch. 'I'm just doing my job. Your flares are out of date.'

'You'd be out of date if you didn't have that uniform. And get that fucking clipboard off my boat. It's not a fucking table, mate.'

I've seen Salt carry on like this before. Marine park reserve meetings. Grievous setting nets over his. Grievous going near the flathead spot when we are already there. Anything to do with Grievous at all really. The thing is, Salt doesn't actually lose his temper, he *cultivates* his temper. Today, he was trying to extract maximum entertainment out of the inevitable infringement notice.

'Do you have a ship's whistle or gas horn?'

'I can whistle quite satisfactorily thank you.'

'A person's whistle is not enough, sir. Do you have a mechanical means of making a noise?'

'Fuckin' oath. It's called punching something like you in the head.'

Trevor crossed another box. 'Can I have your date of birth please?'

This was just too much. 'Can I drive this car away now?'

'No, you can't sir. I observed you approaching the landing –'

'Oh. You *observed*, didya?'

'And now we must complete this interview. Can you give me your date of birth please?'

'Can't remember. Too young at the time. Hey – was your father a Dutchman?'

And on it went. I began to feel sorry for Trevor because Salt was enjoying himself.

'I've only been done for assault once – and that was a CALM officer, twenty years ago,' he told me as we drove away, the infringement notice already on the floor of his car. 'Pity really, I only shoved the guy. Could have really gone to town on the bastard and got the same charge.'

Every old man in the car park waved. They've never done that before. It must have made their day. Salt pulled out his mobile phone as he neared the main road. 'Now. Let's ring the shop and tell them we're bringin' in a box of crabs.'

INTERVIEW WITH THE
FISHERWOMAN, MS MER

I drove out to meet a Windy Harbour fisherwoman on a day when gales and hailstones battered the whole south-west of the continent.

'Trayback Landcruiser. White.' Ms Mer said to me on the phone that she would meet me by the caretaker's shed. I drove along a puddle track past the colourful fishing shacks that stood side by side like uncertain teenagers, until I found her.

'It's the wild woman of Borneo!' she said, leaning out of the ute and taking off her black wraparound sunnies. I could have returned the compliment. Ms Mer was older than she sounded on the phone but her eyes were clear, pure blue like a sun-glad sea. She'd spent so many years at sea that her irises could have been made of the stuff but there was also a bit of steel in there and something else, a humanity, a steady reckoning, kindness. Under her beanie, snow-white hair stuck out in little tufts.

We rumbled past more shacks. 'They keep all us professionals out the back here, out of sight,' she told me later. 'Right at the end of the track. We have to keep all our gear out of sight too, in case it offends the reccies.' She meant the recreational anglers, inland farmers or city dwellers who lease shacks for their holidays. Solar panels perched on reccie roofs like raptors and hot-water systems were wrapped in tarps for the winter to keep out the salt spray. Signs were nailed by the front doors: *Gone Fishin'*, *Hideaway*, *Merv and Averils Castle* or *To the Manor Prawn*.

I was impressed by the lack of signage to Ms Mer's shack. That and the monster of a diesel Lister chugging away in the shed. 'Gotta have it. There's no mains power out here. I need it to make ice mainly.' She makes block ice to keep the fish cool. 'Been through a few of those motors since 1971, three, maybe four ...'

Her garden was smooth beach stones and succulents. Long white socks hung in the garage next to her 'changing room' where the fishers got out of their smelly gear. A carpeted ramp led to the door of her house. She showed me into a room with huge windows where I looked out over sand dunes to the island sitting in a blustery, choppy sea.

Inside the living room there were many shelves of books: hymn books, Lynda la Plante, more crime fiction, Australiana, Reader's Digests, Hammond Innes, poetry. High on one shelf was a yellowed photograph of a young Ms Mer and a fellow nurse from the Vietnam War, grinning into the camera with urchin innocence the way people do in black and white photographs. The Vietnamese child on the stretcher was swathed in sheets and bandages and smiling too.

The Everhot was firing and beneath it two lizards lolled on the warm tiles. A polished kettle hummed on the hotplate. She turned off the radio. 'No good news anyway.' A ticking clock. The roar and roar of that wild sea.

'Cuppa tea? Coffee?'

'I'd love a coffee. Missed out this morning.'

She sniffed when I said I wanted sugar. 'Sugar!' She hunted around for some. 'I don't have sugar in anything. Never have liked the stuff.'

Ms Mer had made barley, bacon and mushroom soup, some coleslaw, pickled beetroot and a plateful of crumbed herring morsels and she placed it all on the table along with some slices of bread and butter. She sat down opposite me, the teabag still dangling from her cup, and fixed me with her blue eyes. She'd taken off her beanie and her white hair framed her like a pixie cap. 'I hope you like the soup. You're not vegan or anything?'

'I'll eat anything.'

'I'm not such a good cook,' she shrugged and smiled.

'This is lovely! It's a feast.' I broke apart the crumbed herring with my fingers.

'Never married, you know. Got out of that one nicely, hey? Never was a man who could cook and clean for me while I went fishing. I don't really care about houses. Houses are just places where us fishers live when we're not aboard a boat.'

She showed me a photograph of a classic West Australian fishing boat, slung up on a lift and about to be launched, surrounded by men in flannelette shirts. 'My old boat, the plankie, I sold her and bought the one I got now. That's just after I bought her. Fibreglass. *Tupperware Girl*, I call her. Not a plank boat. Plankies are a lot of work. When you get them out the water each year you gotta paint them, caulk them again ...'

When Ms Mer was two years old and living on the island, her father would put her in a wicker basket and lower her on a rope down the long walls of granite to the groper hole. He was a strong man and a lighthouse keeper. He would climb down, once he'd safely deposited his child in the nestle of rocks, and together they burleyed up crabs and abalone roe.

Some of the groper were as big as him. He'd climb back up the rocks with the tracer over his shoulder, hauling the monster after him. 'We used to eat fish every day. That and rabbits. Loads of rabbits on Eclipse Island. Austin only came out every few weeks with supplies; firewood, kero, flour, all that stuff, so we ate whatever was there.' Her childhood was spent on the lighthouse islands, from Eclipse Island on the south coast, to the Northern Territory.

The family also worked sharking at Hamelin Bay and rarely went past the island for prey. It is a popular holiday spot and I think netting is now banned there. 'So many sharks!' She chuckled. 'Right where everyone swam and mucked about.'

She showed me a photograph of her as a kid, surrounded in shark carcasses slung from racks and lying in the sand at her feet. Old photos of huge sharks, the images peeled at the edges, sometimes a date and some other details neatly typed on a separate piece of paper and glued beneath the fish – I see these pictures often when talking to the older fishers. Far from macho posings, the commercial fishers tend to take pictures of women wearing shady hats and aprons or children with bleached, wild hair sitting astride a monster that they hooked off the beach or dragged, tail first, out of the salmon net. Women and their daughters have always been part of the action. 'I was snigging salmon up the beach when I was two years old,' said Ms Mer.

TOUGH GUY

Nails has a fearsome reputation. Everything about him is carved hard and grave and he's attractive in a flinty sort of way. Faces like his stared from eighteenth century daguerreotype images.

I had been working with Salt for one inlet season when I met Nails and saw that he was one of those blokes who'll not acknowledge a woman in a boat. I don't think I've ever even seen Nails look sideways at me aboard, let alone say hello. There's some kind of code there I don't understand. But once he'd pulled his boxes of fish from the deck and trudged through the silty shallows in his waders, dropped the boxes on the back of his ute, he would come through the paperbarks to say gidday.

He didn't stoop to that, the first time I saw him, hunkered down at a card table outside the maritime festival. He was collecting signatures to counter the latest campaign against the inlet fishermen. He was pissed off anyway and didn't want my cup of tea, wasn't interested in answering questions about the petition. Like granite, he sat there all day and didn't even get a drink of water.

As he stepped from the paperbarks this day, I saw the thermos in his hand. 'So you *do* drink tea then?'

He shook his head, took two fingers from the open mouth of the flask. They were all white and swollen and flaky.

'Cobbler. Oh. That must have hurt.'

Fishermen hold with the theory that keeping a cobbler-stung finger in hot water will ease the pain.

'Didn't feel it go in,' he laughed. 'Didn't feel it come out either.'

In the afternoon it was time to set the nets again. Severe weather warnings were spraying from the radio. Salt and I decided to pack up the camp and go back to Albany, rather than have nets full of weed dragging us around the inlet in the morning. We passed Nails at the rubbish tip and he pulled over.

'Going home,' Salt said.

'Yeah, Unruly took off too,' he said. 'Jordie fucked off to Perth. No one's fishing tonight. Guess I'm the only crazy bastard around here.' He drove off with a wave.

'He'll be happy anyway, gettin' the place to himself,' said Salt.

He went down the road a bit further, then stopped.

'Bugger it. If he can fish, I can.'

Nails' truck was wedged into the paperbarks by the shore, laden with two big iceboxes, his elastic-sided boots stashed neatly under the tray, out of the rain. Out on the inlet I could see the low sun whitening his wake and the fluorescent green of his raincoat, just past the little island.

We launched the boat and I started the motor. Then I had to start it again.

'Did you turn that thing off?'

'No. It just stopped.'

It sputtered out again. I started it one more time and we ran for a few hundred metres before she stopped for good.

'Give me a go.' Salt stumbled over the nets. He yanked and cursed for five minutes and then looked straight up into the squall. Squalls only ever hit us when the motor fails, we are setting net, or the bung is lost. I've never known it to be any other way.

The wind blew us towards the island. Salt threw me an oar and we both tried to punt against the wind to the car park. His words, shouted into the mad blow, went something like this:

'Push away from starboard, push the bow around. Keep 'er straight. Don't touch the gunwales with the oar, you're pushing the bow around too much. C'mon, you can do it. You know what you are doing. Push the fucking bow around. Don't lose that oar. It'll get stuck in the mud and you'll lose the bastard. Stop pushing the bow around ...'

By this time, Salt had run out of breath and the oars made no difference.

'Why don't we just blow over to the island and then row back when this storm is over?'

'Because we'll be there all bloody night! Oh, *just let me do it*.' He punted harder against the wind and I threw down my oar because we were hurtling towards the island anyway. Being harangued like that makes me mutinously useless.

We blew to the island, the boat side-on to the wind like a sail.

'There's some rocks ahead. Do you want to lift the motor?'

'I don't give a flying fuck about that fucking piece of shit.'

The prop bunted over the submerged rocks. The boat edged into the reeds and stopped. I thought, I've always wanted to visit this island and we've always been too busy and now look, here I am.

I stepped out of the boat and into the reedy skirts of the island. Salt didn't see me because he was hunched over the innards of the outboard. I scrambled past a tea-tree thicket and found myself in a flat, stone clearing, thick with orange and khaki lichen, surrounded in soft white paperbarks and tea-trees. Around the stone lay swathes of brilliant green moss, glistening with rain and studded with tiny red flowers.

I wanted to stay there forever.

The horizon brightened with sunlight and the wind and the rain ceased their harrying. I went back to the boat.

Salt was replacing the lid to the outboard, cursing.

'I'll row back.' I fitted the oars to the rowlock.

'Yeah, we'll give it a miss today.'

Nails rounded the island in his big flat-bottomed punt.

'I'll row,' said Salt and got to the thwart before I could sit down. 'Haven't rowed for ages. Like rowing.'

So he rowed and I stood at the stern feeling useless again. Nails motored closer and I waved him over, hoping for a tow.

'What the hell are yer doin'?' Salt sure was grumpy that day. 'Never call another fisherman over! Fuck!' He rowed harder.

Nails was just ahead. I smiled but he didn't look at me. He asked Salt what was wrong with the motor. I scrambled up to the bow and pulled the rope out from under the boxes and anchors and fuel tank. I threw him the rope. Then I remembered the big U-bolt on the end. 'Watch out. There's a weight on it.' To his credit, he ducked.

Back on shore the two fishermen spent half an hour talking about busted outboards and cobbler and yelloweye mullet. Nails glanced at my hair hanging all kelpy and dripping. 'Probly should let you fellas go and get dry.'

I drove. Salt got out his mobile phone. 'Dusty. I wanna talk to you about that outboard you sold me for a pup ... yeah ... The prop's not going around enough to get us underway. You know what I mean? I tried turning the bastard by hand but it just doesn't go round fast enough. Gotta crank handle you can sell me?'

CAN'T KILL HIM WITH AN AXE

We set some whiting net along the cockle banks. Salt threw over the last buoy and checked his bearings so we could find the net in the early morning.

'That sand spit is under the hill that looks like a tit.' He turned around and surveyed the flat landscape ringing the inlet on the northern side. 'And bugger all that way.'

He grabbed the rope. I gunned the motor, heading for the car park. The problem was that Salt had fumbled and not grabbed the rope at all. The forward momentum of the boat sent him into an amazing spear manoeuvre, a kind of horizontal pole vault, his body straight as a ladder, over the thwart, over the deck and he landed on his head on a pile of chains at my feet. There he stayed, his eyes wide open and the colour of curdled milk.

I fumbled about for the kill switch. Then I changed my mind. What if he was badly injured and the cranky outboard wouldn't start again? So I yanked the gear into neutral instead. If he didn't come to, there was no way I was getting him out of the boat. He must weigh thirteen, fourteen stone. We were sixty kilometres from the nearest town. I'd have to winch him and the boat onto the trailer and drive miles and miles to a nursing post with him bouncing around on the deck.

It took a long minute for him to regain consciousness and another ten before he was able to get to his feet and pat himself down. He thought he may have broken a rib. The rest of the Irwin's trip was peppered with Panadol and pain for Salt. He had to sleep on the floor of the shack like the rest of us – getting in and out of the swag must have hurt.

A week later we were dropping pots in Oyster Harbour, with the mistaken idea there may have been crabs there.

'I reckon you gave me a good kicking when I was knocked out,' said Salt, feeling his ribs. 'It's still bloody sore.'

I didn't say anything but scanned the seagrass for a pot we'd lost, and smiled.

'I take it from your silence that I'm right.'

Of course he wasn't but, 'It does sound appealing sometimes.'

Accidents can happen in the most banal of circumstances. Just a fumble with a rope, dropping a spanner, fiddling with a car radio ... Salt on his lonesome in a boat can be dangerous. After he dropped me off on Breaksea Island, he was knocked out when he fell over. He woke to the big Quintrex slewing around in the swell. I think he's glad I'm around, mostly. The day I was there to put his nose back together and call an ambulance could have turned out rather different.

I can make mistakes though, and Salt falling over in boats is often my fault. I missed the starboard channel marker once, tipping Salt into the life jackets and anchors in the bow as I ploughed straight into the sandbank. One night Salt was sitting on the pile of nets as we returned home from the Sound. He slid sideways when I broached the boat on a channel wave and he fell against the gunwale with one arm trailing in the water. I kept going, thinking he would right himself, wondering why he stayed there. He told me later that his raincoat was collecting water and turning him into a sea anchor.

OYSTERMEN

Sometimes, late at night, the only other fishers around in the Sound are Grievous, and Gawain checking his leatherjacket pots. Catching leatheries is not his day job though. Gawain is also the director of a local seafood company. I see Gawain and Kilpatrick at the Sunday markets every week but the source of the creamy, salty oysters that they sell has always been a bit of a mystery to me.

The first time I saw the oyster farm from a distance I thought it was a conglomerate of old wire fences that a farmer had built into the sea to stop cows from crossing paddocks along the beach. I had no idea it was an oyster farm. Then, one morning picking up nets on the east side of the harbour, I saw the barge out there and the figures of men in bright orange rain coats moving about the 'fences'.

I asked Gawain if I could go out on the barge with them and he rang me at six o'clock one morning. 'We're leaving in twenty minutes, Sarah. Are you coming out?'

I drove down to the Emu Point shipyards where ancient wooden boats lined up with newer steel jobs, past the seafood restaurant, the chandler's shop and the slipway manager's sheds. Gawain had the tractor hooked up to the barge. Men donned wetsuits, getting ready for the trip.

'Sarah, have you met Diesel?' Gawain introduced me to the crew: Diesel, a bluff, hulking, fisherman sort; Turk, tattooed with sunnies and a long beard; Jason, whippet-lean in his sealskin, beanie and sunnies. The two German backpackers in bright orange sou'-westers, Chris and John, nodded hello. Kilpatrick was staying to shuck oysters in the shed.

'Where's yer boots?' Diesel said to one of the Germans. 'You got any gumboots mate?' He looked at me and rolled his eyes. 'Wellingtons? Galoshes? Ahh. Whatever. You right then, everyone? Ready. Let's go.'

Once the boat was launched, Gawain jumped in and Diesel dropped the propeller and started her up. We backed into the shallow waters around the service jetty. 'Tide's still going down,' muttered Diesel. 'Better get a move on.' Despite the early hour, a wind blew in from the east. Two men stood in the water on the sandbar with fishing rods. We motored towards Green Island.

Diesel and Turk lit up tailor-mades in the shelter of the cabin and then put on their white cotton gloves. Diesel looked like he had always been a fisherman. He has been working the oysters for ten years now but before that he was a diesel mechanic. I looked at his boots. He wore diving boots with white gumboot tops elastic-banded around them, like gaiters.

'What are they all about?' I asked him.

'I invented them myself,' he said. 'You see, all the stingray wounds I've ever heard of go in at the ankle or the top of the foot, or the sides. Never the bottom. So this is my protection. Don't know if the theory's right but I've never been barbed yet.'

'We get those little purple stingrays,' Gawain explained to me. 'Those buggers with the pink undersides. They're the worst ones.'

'Cobbler?'

The men shuddered in unison. 'We don't talk about cobbler.'

The oyster racks are lined up in hundreds of rows in the still, shallow waters of the eastern side. There is something very beautiful about their barnacled repetitions. Held together with sticks the size of tomato stakes, black rubber bands and rope, the racks reminded me of bamboo pathways through some kind of Asian water village. Their rickety regularity and the olive-hued beauty of tidal Oyster Harbour make the structures a kind of art.

The barge was loaded with trays of oysters that had already

been graded for size and were being returned to the racks. Diesel steered the barge into a channel just wide enough and killed the motor.

'Watch out for blue-rings,' warned Gawain.

I'd forgotten all about the blue-ringed octopus. When we were kids swimming at Emu Point, much mention was made not to fiddle with underwater containers or grottos where the deadly critters lived.

'Do you get many here?'

'Yeah, we get a few. Years ago, we were getting ten, twenty a day in the cages. Bloody awful. Then that hundred-year flood came through. Remember that? All the fresh water coming out of the rivers got rid of them. But they're coming back now.'

Diesel, Turk, Chris and Gawain jumped overboard into knee-deep water. Chris held the barge in position against the wind. Jason stayed on the deck with John and started throwing out the trays to them. The three waders clipped the cages full of oysters onto the racks.

'Hey, Gawain, did I tell yer about my blue-ring dream?'

I wouldn't recognise Jason in his civvies. His wetsuit, beanie and sunglasses made him a deckie creature. 'The night after I got that one on me leg, I dreamt there was one on me arm and I kept trying to shake it off, flaring up its bastard rings all blue at me. Shit. What a dream.'

'Sounds like a nightmare,' Gawain sighed over a broken tray clip and said, 'lacky band, please.'

'Oh, nah,' Jason said, handing him an elastic. 'Nah, just a dream.'

'I've never seen one before, and I've lived here all my life,' I said.

Turk handed me a stake with a blue-ringed octopus clinging to it. 'Here's one I prepared earlier.' The tiny, slimy creature with electric blue marks jumped off the stick and slid into the sea around the legs of the men.

'Lacky band, please.'

The deckies threw the trays and lacky bands to the waders

until the deck was clear except for remnants of broken cages, barnacles and algae. Turk kept straightening up in the water and rubbing the small of his spine. I could see he suffered the same back as Salt.

Once the trays were done, the oystermen turned to harvesting. Diesel started up the motor again and moved the barge into another row further to the west, where the burnt out hill loomed brindle against silver water. He dropped into the water and counted the oysters in a random tray. 'Forty-five.'

Some swift mathematics flew around between the crew.

'Forty-five per unit?'

'Four dozen.'

'Fifty dozen times four dozen is …' Jason was onto it.

'Nah, fifty times forty-five!'

It was all too fast for me. Within minutes the crew worked out how many units they needed to load for the Perth markets.

Black bream swam around Turk's feet, feeding on the nutrients that his movements were stirring up, amongst the ferny brown weed and seagrass.

'They're a good size too,' Turk said. 'Should get that line out!'

'Turk, you got a fisherwoman on board! Don't tell her where the bream are.'

'Do you chuck a line in ever?' I asked, trying not to eye those fat bream any more than was respectable.

'Nah,' Turk said, grinning at his boss. 'We're here to work, mate, not go fishing.'

After about forty minutes of throwing racks of oysters up to the men on board, who stacked them neatly against the cabin, the day's quota was fulfilled. By then the wind and the sun had opened up the clouds. The men climbed into the boat and Diesel started up the motor again.

'What species are they, these oysters?'

'Sydney rock oysters. They don't spawn in these cold waters, so they don't get away. We're not allowed to use Pacific oysters here because they might get away. But South Australia uses them, so I dunno. These ones we are bringing in now, they're bistro oysters, a bit smaller. They'll get graded and sent off today.'

'These are from Carnarvon aren't they?' Diesel asked Gawain.

'Sydney rock oysters from Carnarvon?'

'Yeah, I think they got bred up there.'

'How many did you pick up today?'

'Two thousand dozen.'

Diesel found his shucking knife. 'Grab one of those things.'

I picked out a nice fat oyster. He prised it open while Turk held the steering wheel for him, flicked the top shell overboard and turned the oyster flesh over in its base. Then he handed it to me.

There is nothing quite like a fresh oyster, with the liquor still liquoring and all that salty sweet creaminess going on.

Back at the boat yards, Gawain backed the tractor down to the ramp and Diesel drove the boat straight onto the jinker. The others piled out and headed for the hose, past the neatly swept piles of barnacle shells below the sorting racks, to rinse off their gear before their nine o'clock coffee break.

Oystermen.

PORTRAIT

He is the son of the son of a fisherman. A small man, his beard grows down to his chest, flecked with grey. I don't think I've ever seen the hair on top of his head: a beanie covers him up, or a cap, or maybe even a cowboy hat on the weekends when he isn't fishing. He wears polarised sunnies that give off a blue-green hue. I see myself in peacock colours at the truck depot unloading fish into the refrigerator trucks for the city market. He's a few years older than me. His nose looks like it has been boiled in rum. His voice is gravelly from the smokes. He wears skinny black jeans, a blue flannelette shirt that exposes his tattooed forearms and singlet. Fishing boots.

He is stalking around his boat trailer on an early boat ramp morning. He wears olive green waders and he is muttering. I can see he feels like shouting but no fisherman shouts when the Fisheries start going through his nets and his catch with measuring sticks. In another life, he might have been a jockey, a racing car driver, one of those guys who change your tyres or fix the problem plumbing. But he's not. His dad was a fisherman and so is he. He probably did his apprenticeship during primary school. He never gave a shit about getting an education or observing the social contract. These trappings of society would never have served him anyway. He was born into the cycles of nature. He has a code that he honours and it works for him.

When Salt and I are fishing in the channel, we've come across him. He will brandish a knife that looks suspiciously like the Asian machetes seized by Fisheries up north; the ones shaped from car springs and sharpened, the handles wrapped in string and fish leather. Salt grudgingly respects him, because he knew his dad, and his dad's dad. He could exist in any era. He could be one of those sealers who lurked around here in the 1820s. Bearded, lean, tattooed, full of a stringy, muscular hunger; an anarchic, five foot tall package of a fisherman.

INTERVIEW WITH A FISHERWOMAN 2

Ms Mer asked how Salt was going. I said he was still fighting with Grievous.

'That's been goin' on for a while now. He's a bandit, that Salt! Oh yes, he's been a wild one in his day.'

'I've seen him go off once or twice.'

'You shoulda seen him during Fisheries meetings!'

'I've been in the same room as him during a marine parks meeting ...' When Salt starts blathering at meetings I feel strangely protective of him and embarrassed at the same time.

'Yes, the marine parks ...' We finished our lunch and she tidied the kitchen. 'Thought you might like to go for a drive.'

I've not spent much time on this part of the coast. It's up near where the Southern and Indian oceans meet and jammed between two limestone capes. The winds are different – a nor'-wester here can blow for weeks during the winter.

'You must need good moorings,' I said, as we stared out at the grey sea through a trail of cracks in the Landcruiser's windscreen. Five fishing boats were rocking madly in the swell that crashed over the reef and into the little harbour.

'Oh yes,' she said. 'That's why we don't like leaving them there over the winter. Gotta keep at the moorings all the time.' She'd put on her beanie and wraparounds again and out of the kitchen she appeared like any old man of the sea, but when she spoke her voice was gentle, tough and female. I wondered if I could live her life. When she was my age, she'd already been fishing commercially for twenty years.

'How do you fuel up your boat? There's no jetties here.'

'We take out fuel drums in the dinghy.'

'And all the ice?'

'Yeah, the ice too.'

Ms Mer drove over the hill past the lighthouse to Salmon Beach. 'Here it is!' She swept her arm across the horizon. 'West! Straight out there. Leeuwin.'

'The Cape?'

'Yeah. My boat's over there, at Augusta. I woulda brought her down this week, if my back hadn't laid me up.'

'How long does it take?'

'Augusta to Windy? About five hours. Some blokes would flog it but I take my time. Saves fuel.'

'Is this where you catch salmon?'

'Nah! I catch them with my neighbour, up the other end near the Gardner River. Though I saw some down by Cathedral Rock the other day. I was sitting up in the car park and saw this whole school of salmon go single file, like Indians, out to sea through the little channel there.'

They'd tried catching salmon at Salmon Beach. It took two days to walk the catch back over the dunes because they couldn't get a truck down there. 'Never again,' she grinned.

The wind was brutal at wild Salmon Beach. Intermittent sunshine sent the water's strained surface into a blinding mess of white.

'You used to be able to land an aeroplane on this beach,' she said. 'Actually, I think someone did!' Then the Department of Environment and Conservation planted the dunes with introduced grasses, to protect them, she told me. They protected them so well that two more dunes appeared and now the beach was a tiny strip of sand. 'You can hardly walk along it.' The marram grass ran away up into the bush, waving against the native scrub-like flags.

Later, back in her kitchen, Ms Mer began to explain the obstacles that she must overcome if she were to continue fishing. One of the leasehold conditions on her home is that she mustn't spend more than twelve months away from commercial fishing. 'If I do, I'm supposed to pull down the house and return the block to its natural state.' She blew lightly. 'So I'd have to sell the licence too and then sell the house lease with it. There's all these things happening – the marine parks, the review – all wild cards. We just don't know where we are at the moment. We can't sell any licences until we know what's going on.

'The Fisheries are gonna do this review soon and then we'll know where we are. They don't seem to know when they are gonna do it. They don't even know what time period they will be reviewing or the cut-off catch rates – or they're not saying. I've got a good enough history on my boat. I've been fishing since 1971. But they might decide that I'm not killing enough fish for a certain time period and take my licence off of me. At the moment it's all up in the air.

'Then there's the marine parks. The government has just changed their proposal and now they want this patch out here.' She pointed out the window.

'But won't all the reserves be three or more nautical miles out?'

She looked at me. 'We don't fish any closer in. We're finished if that goes through.'

'But you can still fish the inlets?'

'Yeah, while they're open waters. Six months of the year. See, the line fishing is my main kind of fishing now. Snapper, dhuies, kingies, that sort of fish.'

'What about the petitions?'

Ms Mer's patch has recently been subject to another recreational fishing group targeting the netters.

'Oh that idiot!' She laughed. 'It's just constant, isn't it, keeping up with blokes like that. I'd like Fisheries to start jumping on those amateurs who are selling fish out of Windy Harbour too! You wouldn't believe the amount of fish they're pulling out of here.'

Ms Mer had her arms resting on the table with her hands

folded together, just like a farmer does when he comes in for a cup of tea. 'This sittin' around is drivin' me mad, you know. I'm normally up and at it by four thirty, five, in the morning. I want to get up to Augusta and bring the boat back and get out fishing. I'm fine sitting down, which is why I can drive around like always but I just can't bloody walk. Can't do anything. Read some good books though. There's so many things to sort out, the boat, the Fisheries review, the marine parks thing ... but first, first there is my back operation. And my deckie's gone AWOL.'

Despite the limbo period imposed upon her, it seemed that nobody told Ms Mer that she couldn't go to sea, build her own boats, run lobster pots or catch shark for a living. She shrugs off any thought of a cosseted life. Theatre nurse in a civilian hospital during wartime, busting the gearbox in a heavy swell with a gang hook through her foot ... ('They've got boltcutters at the nursing post now. Didn't have them *that* day.') They sound like tales of derring-do and adventure; to the woman who sits in front of me now, amid her placemats and crocheted rugs, it is the only life she has led, and a fine one too.

BEGINNING THE CONCLUSION

I know how to do this. It is late afternoon and the wind is up. I turn the dinghy in a long arc into windward slop and watch for Salt to gather himself. I point the boat for the paperbarks. He doesn't need to flick directions at me as he stands amidships but still he flicks the back of his hand towards the shore. A digital Rosetta Stone for lesser folk. It's me at the tiller. *I know how to do this now, Salt,* I think as I roar up to the paperbarks, lift the motor when we hit the shallow coral grounds, ease the throttle.

I can see another little boat moored in the flooded trees, its rope threaded through branches, the outboard out of the water and tilted to the right. The dark flash of a solar panel through the forest and a smudge of camp fire smoke above. I work the tinny along a bit. 'There's a boat in there,' I say to Salt. 'They'll run into our nets tonight if we set there.' Get closer to where the afternoon sun bleaches the trees to ghostly white, full lock to the nor'-west, pull the gear astern, full lock to the sou'-east, straighten up, back in the boat to where the big old bream lurk. The mountains are a blue-grey bruise on the sky. Salt fiddles with the tangled buoys. Our wake arrives, shwishing against submerged trees and onto the sandy shore. Then it is only the jaded cawing of crows, the thump and crack of the swell outside the bar, the soft throb of the motor as we play out nets. The mushroomy scent of nets and sweet flowers over the water. A sentinel sea eagle hangs above me, watching.

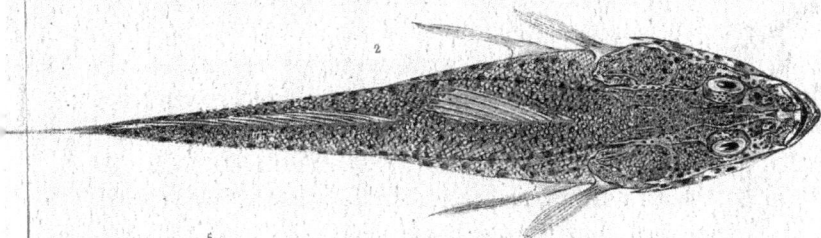

GAFFER-TAPED WADERS

'There's no future in this for me,' I told Salt as we sat outside at a plastic table at the fishing camp.

'What do you mean?'

'You know.'

Inshore and estuarine commercial fishing is played out in the magenta light of dawn and dusk but it is also the most visible kind of fishing. Our interaction with the public is daily, whether it be at boat ramps, beaches, the bream banks, or selling the produce at the markets. It also seems to be the most criticised form of commercial fishing by anglers and other special interest groups. The irony here is that small-scale, inshore fishing has historically shown the least impact on fish stocks and the general ocean environment. The guys you *don't* see at the boat ramp, trawling the ocean floors off the Continental Shelf with huge operational overheads, by-catch wastage and quotas, are the ones who I would examine more closely for environmental concerns. Estuarine and inshore fishers tend to have few overheads and work a small operation. It's also in the best interests of local fishing families to keep the fish stocks healthy, so they can return the next season and their children can inherit their licences, through the 'Grandfather Clause'.

On the south coast, the gentrification of inshore waters and the social shying away from primary industry to embrace the more profitable sea-change real estate and leisure industries mean that small-scale commercial inshore fishers are really copping it. Estuarine and small wetline licences are being bought back by the Government, killed off by quota restrictions or simply taken away by Fisheries Department reviews when there is no evidence of a licence being worked hard enough. Recreational fishers run populist campaigns on the internet and in local fishing tackle shops to rid certain areas of commercial fishing, their argument often plonked on top of a misleading environmental plinth.

In July 2010, the State Minister for Fisheries announced the closure of commercial netting from Busselton to Augusta, putting eleven fishing families out of work. Although they will be compensated for their licences, the natural history knowledge and the cultural heritage of these fishers deserts the beaches with them. The Fisheries Department conceded that the decision to ban commercial netting on that coast was based primarily on appeasing beachgoers and anglers and had nothing to do with conserving fish stocks. In fact, the kind of fish that were netted on the beaches between Busselton and Augusta tended to be small run and bait fish – environmentally sustainable, high in omega-3 oils and very cheap to buy.

There are twenty-five estuarine licensees in the south-west of Western Australia and the Government is trying to cut them down to fifteen. The licences cannot be sold or leased to anyone else, though this may be subject to change in the future. The owner of an estuarine licence must be present during netting. None of these guys are getting any younger.

'But there's more isn't there,' I ploughed on, reckless and a little annoyed that Salt wouldn't commiserate with me being stuck working for him. 'Look at what is going on in Oyster Harbour. There are folk who've spent a million bucks on a house overlooking the sea who don't want to be woken up by a dirty old two-stroke at five in the morning. They go to Greece or Thailand if they want to experience *authentic* fishermen. And those other guys, the ones who buy one-fifty horsepower jet boats and use it for a black bream anglers' competition? They don't want you catching *their* fish. These people have the power of wealth behind them, more than old-school fishermen. They'll just import fish, or farm it, or something.'

'It's not over yet. We'll be here for a long time yet.' Salt refused to believe my argument but still a fat tear rolled down his cheek. 'How many anti-commercial campaigns have you seen since you started fishing?'

'Oh, three?'

'Well, we've been dealing with them for years. And the government. They haven't stopped us yet.'

Maybe he's right, and crusty old fishermen in waders with gaffer tape covering the holes in the bum will continue to fish the harbours around here for another century.

These fishing families are the greatest observers of aquatic change and diversity in the Great Southern. They've been decades, generations, watching and interacting with nature. It's another reason though, why I sit outside this shack talking to Salt, why I get up before dawn to punt a boat smelling of fish guts out into the inlet; and why I struggle with the two-stroke and put up with the same stupid crab jokes and get scared stiff at night surfing the channel home and pick sea lice from between my toes and get mutinous but never really, truly quit. When I pick apart the politics of this work, I get an ominous sense of the industry's fragility. Perhaps it is just that, like farmers, commercial fishers have always felt endangered by outside forces beyond their control and I am daily exposed to their woes. But although I feel close to the tribal ties of these south coast fishers, I am still an outsider, an observer, and the social historian in me worries that fishing lifestyles on the south coast are dying of a thousand cuts; and that the stories and knowledge will go with them.

SARAH AND THE POET

I met a poet from Tipperary. A man in his fifties; his humour, his wisps of hair and pale, elfin face made him a different creature from anyone I'd ever met. I wanted to tell him that, despite his bemoaning the status of poetry in Australia, clandestine visitors to one of the isolated fishing shacks I frequent had stolen only my copy of Philip Larkin's *Collected Poems*. They could have shot holes in the rainwater tank or taken the gas bottle or generator. But no ... a book of poetry.

He nodded slowly. 'Larkin. They showed good taste.'

'I thought so too.'

'I heard that you are a fisherwoman,' he said.

'Yes. We work the estuaries and beaches with nets, in a little boat.'

He took his time during the conversation. He looked distracted and stared across the table at something or someone. 'You look like you are strong.'

'I am.'

'I shall tell my wimpy public servant friends in Ireland all about you,' he said. 'How did you begin this fishing life?'

'I grew up here. Then there were tuna fishermen and whalers, hard men, and it was a woman's job to serve them beer or shovel the fish in the factories. I did that for a while but I wanted to work on a boat. One day I started working for Salt.'

'Do you argue on the boat? It must be hard, sometimes ...'

'We argue, often. It's a small boat.'

'But you work for this man, because ... you must feel some affection for him.'

'Yes. Yes. I do feel affection for him.'

He shook my hand goodbye but then stopped and said that he would like one day to read this book, this *Salt Story*.

AVALON

Smoke lies low. The burning season has begun. Plumes rise from the dark hills and curl over the inlet, creeping along the country and fingering across the water. One border of the inlet is still smouldering from a controlled burn: black stalks of trees with their ochre, scorched leaves, grasstrees already sprouting new shoots, golden light. The eastern side is emerald green, regrowth from last year's fires. A bald, surprised-looking hill rears above the sand dunes. Grasses, sedges, reeds curb the waters.

Kermit was caught last year – setting his nets on the midnight prior to the commercial season opening at Irwin's. The confiscation of his gear, boat, catch and a fine ten times the value of his catch nearly took him out of circulation. It hurt anyway.

'They did let us set at midnight one year,' Salt told me. 'Ohh! It was bedlam! Everyone sat around in the shack here, drinkin' and carryin' on. Come midnight and we were all out on the water running over each other's nets in the dark, fouling props and wreckin' nets and gettin' into barneys. Funny. Prissed as crickets we were and the night as black as pitch.'

We camp in a salmon fisherman's shack by the roaring, reef-strewn ocean of Foul Bay. We drive down to the paperbarks to fish the inlet. Evenings we set nets along the cockle banks; two- and quarter-inch mesh for whiting and herring; three- or four-inch for the cobbler and mullet and skippy.

We go back to the shack, where for years the south coast fishermen gathered like migratory birds for the opening of the season. Now it's just us. We light the fire, cook some chops, tomato sauce and bread kind of fare. We drink wine, tell stories, read books and sit on swags on the floor.

I read about Flinders encountering the magic of Kinjarling ('place of rain'), or King George Sound. I am wedged into the corner of the kitchenette and asbestos wall. Stormboy cuddles Digger in his swag under the table. Digger is normally an 'outside' dog and neither dog nor boy can believe their luck. Salt camps near the kitchen sink, mounded upon olive green carpet, playing ringtones on his mobile phone and texting, gradually surrounding himself in a snow of lolly wrappers.

Before dawn, I'm fighting the dog for leg space. Salt puts the kettle on and stumps out into the gloom. Ocean noises thump through the doorway.

At the little paperbark forest, a man gets out of his campervan to watch us launch. He won't talk to me until Salt is present and then tells him all about his pre-retirement vocation selling outboards to fishermen up and down the east coast. He knows all about fishing. Salt humours him and poses for photos while I punt out with an oar, dogged as always by the pelicans.

We pick up the nets.

Cold feet on chequer plate again, warming as the sun rises. Thick fog turns the little island into a mysterious Avalon. Smoke is dense on the water.

Cobbler, huge, angry creatures, their eel tails writhing around their fatal bonds, their slimy mottled skins cool and slippery to the touch, all the colours of the cockle beds.

Snapper, pale pink of dawn skies, iridescent blue spots along their spine, too small, they get thrown back alive.

Yelloweye mullet in the red box give off their intense iodine odour.

Squadrons of opportunistic pelicans come at us out of the

smoke and fog, skidding to a halt alongside the boat. Swans watch from a distance. The elegant snowy egrets are shy too. The inlet – she's closed to the ocean by a quicksandy bar sodden with brine that quivers beneath my feet.

Littered with kelp and strange flotsam, she is a woman-space with womb-soft skies and nacre'd water of pearl.

Back at the shack, we lay the fish into huge iceboxes and shovel crumbly salted ice over them. A late breakfast: the muscular, spiny limbs of broken blue manna crabs, fillets of herring whose heads were chewed off by a shark trapped behind the bar, fat fillets of yellowfin whiting, sea mullet.

REFERENCES

Culotta, Nino (John O'Grady), *Gone Fishin'*, Ure Smith, Sydney, 1962.

Brandenstein, C.G. von, *Nyungar Anew: phonology, text samples and etymological and historical 1500-word vocabulary of an artificially re-created Aboriginal language in the South-West of Australia, Pacific Linguistics*, Pacific Linguisitics, C-99, Australian National University, Canberra, 1988.

Drummond, Sarah, *Seasons of Abundance: a look at the salmon fishing industry of the Albany region*, unpublished report, Albany Public Library, Battye Library, Perth, 2005.

Fletcher, W.F. and Santoro, K. (eds), *State of the Fisheries and the Aquatic Resources Report, 2010–2011*, Government of Western Australia, Department of Fisheries, Perth, 2011.

Heberle, Greg, *Heberle Fishing: Western Australia 1929–2004*, Ocean Publishing, Western Australia, 2006.

Hill, Ernestine, *My Love Must Wait: the story of Matthew Flinders*, Angus and Robertson, Sydney, 1978 (first published 1941).

Hodgkin, E.P. and Clark, R., *Estuarine Studies Series,* Nos 2–7, 1989–1990, available from Environmental Protection Authority, Perth.

Keen, Ian, *Aboriginal Economy and Society: Australia at the threshold of colonisation*, Oxford University Press, Victoria, 2004.

Muir, Jane, *Settlers, Fishers & Allsorts: stories from the South West*, Jane Muir, Perth, 2007.

Neill, Robert, 'Catalogue of Reptiles and Fish Found at King George's Sound', in Appendix 2, *Journal of Expeditions of Discovery into Central Australia, and Overland from Adelaide to King George's Sound, in the Years 1840–1*, Edward John Eyre, University of Adelaide Library, eBooks@Adelaide, 2013; available from: ebooks.adelaide. edu.au/e/eyre/edward_john/e98j.

Scott, Kim and Brown, Hazel, *Kayang and Me*, Fremantle Press, Fremantle, 2013 (first published 2005).

Stubbs, Ches, *I Remember: the memoirs of a whaling skipper*, self-published, date unknown, available from: trove.nla. gov.au/work/12195894.

Williams, Jack in *Ngulak Ngarnk Nidja Boodja: Our Mother, This Land*, Centre for Indigenous History and the Arts, University of Western Australia, Perth, 2000.

Wright, Guy, *Fishing for a Living: the estuarine and beach fisheries of the Western Australian South Coast*, Western Australian Fishing Industry Council, Fremantle, 2012.

ACKNOWLEDGMENTS

To the men, women and children who played a role in the creation of *Salt Story*: Murray Arnold, Paul Benson, Hazel Brown, Harley Coyne, Richard Davy, Judy Dittmer, Jon Doust, John Drummond, Maya Drummond, George Ebbett, Michelle Frantom, Bill Harsley, Selina Hill, Bob Howard, Gareth James, Colin and Robyn Kennedy, Graeme and Nancy Kennedy, Ray Kilpatrick, Christine King, Mark Kleeman, Lynette Knapp, Alex Levack, Morgan Lindberg, Karina Mitchell, Pauline and Ken Mitchell, Carmelita O'Sullivan, Chris Pash, Carol Pettersen, Scott Rogers, Alan Rule, Sheilah Ryan, Kim Scott, Alf and Bev Sharp, Greg Sharp, Terry Sharp, Jimmy Simpson, David Sims, Yann Toussaint, Kathryn Trees, Sally Drummond Wilson, Adam Wolfe, Guy Wright, the oystermen, with thanks for Georgia Richter's keen editorial eye, and special thanks and appreciation to Bill North. My apologies to any I have left out.

Also thanks to: Department of Fisheries, Albany; Department of Indigenous Affairs, Albany; Fremantle Press; University of Western Australia, Albany campus; and the Western Australian Fishing Industry Council.

Special thanks to Sue Morrison, Acting Curator, Fish Section, Aquatic Zoology, Western Australian Museum, and to the museum for their provision of images in this book, which have been drawn from *The Zoology of the Voyage of H.M.S. Erebus & Terror: under the command of Captain Sir James Clark Ross, during the years 1839 to 1843* by Sir James Clark Ross (Sir John Richardson and John Edward Gray (eds), E.W. Janson, England, 1875.

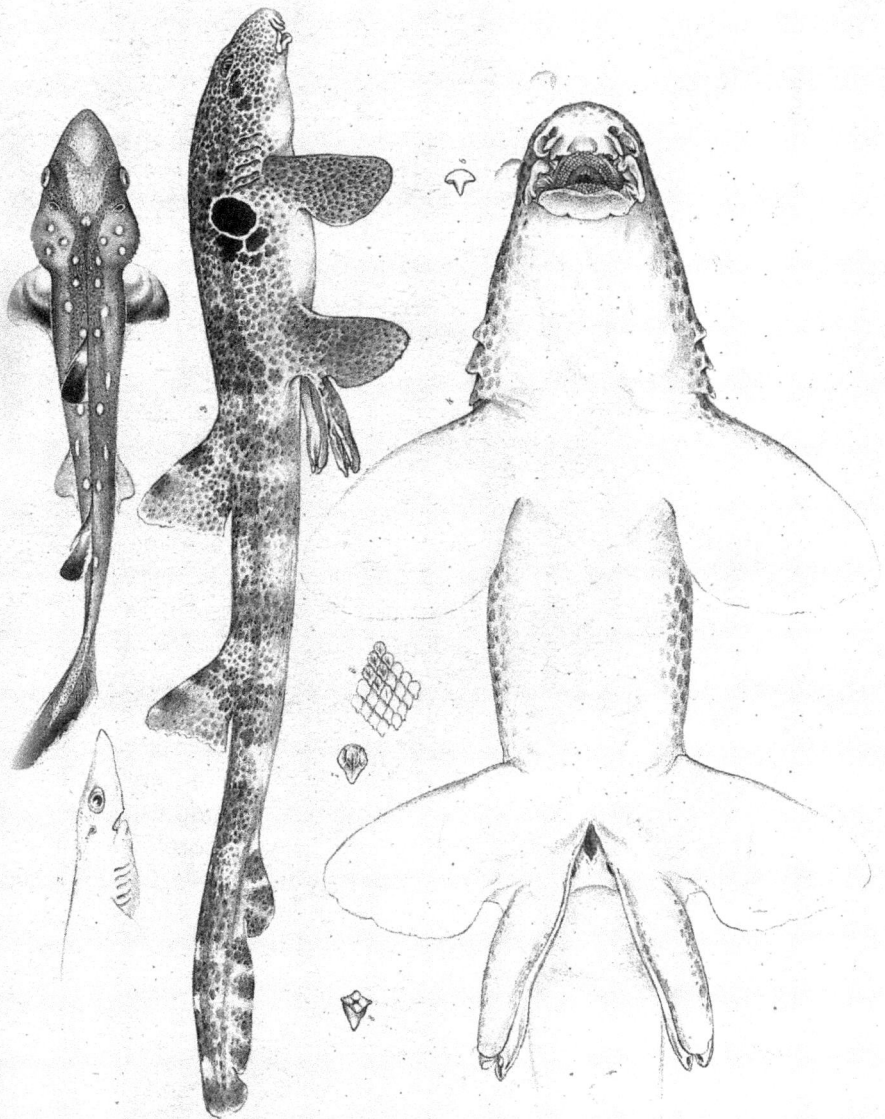

ABOUT THE AUTHOR

Sarah Drummond lives on the south coast of Western Australia. *Salt Story* was shortlisted for the Dobbie Literary Award and the Western Australian Premier's Book Awards. Visit the *Salt Story* photo archive at **sarahdrummond.org**.

ALSO BY SARAH DRUMMOND

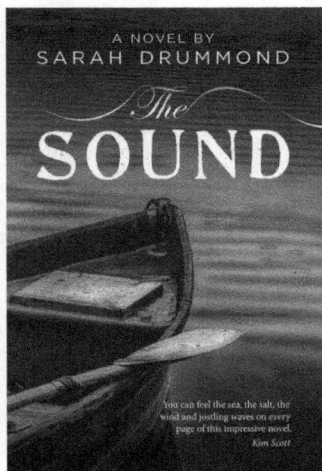

Wiremu Heke of Aramoana joins a sealing boat on a voyage from Tasmania to Western Australia in a quest to avenge the destruction of his village. This is a lawless world, where men from many nations plunder seal colonies and steal women and children from the indigenous communities on the islands and shorelines of Australia's south.

ISBN: 9781925163759 (PB)
EISBN: 9781925163773 (EPUB)

FROM FREMANTLEPRESS.COM.AU

www.ingramcontent.com/pod-product-compliance
Lightning Source LLC
Chambersburg PA
CBHW020532270326
41927CB00006B/549